It is a privilege for me to endorse *Wise Women* [...] very experienced, practical, and spiritual expert [...] management. I know that 80 percent of married [...] will experience widowhood and at least 50 percent will experience divorce. To have women writing to women with sound, practical, expert advice is a necessity, and this book meets that need. I recommend the book highly and trust that God will use it in a significant way in the lives of thousands of women.

RON BLUE
Founder, Ronald Blue Trust

Finally! A complete financial guide anyone can understand—and don't be misled by the title; *Wise Women Managing Money* is great for men too. I kept finding myself surprised, and delighted, that Miriam and Valerie have put the cookies on the lower shelf where even lay*men* can understand these things. They've proved this complex landscape can be navigated by anyone—and from a biblical viewpoint to boot.

JERRY B. JENKINS
Novelist (*Left Behind* and *The Chosen*) and biographer (Billy Graham and many others)

Through the landmark Women Doing Well study, we listened to the voices of over seven thousand women and heard the clear message that women want to "do well." We also heard that women who were fully engaged in their purpose and passion and who were clear on their plan were the most fulfilled and generous! Do you want to be a woman "doing well"? If so, I recommend that you read Miriam Neff and Valerie Hogan's book, *Wise Women Managing Money*. Using an interactive and conversational style, Neff and Hogan travel with you through money topics that today may seem confusing or uninteresting. They are positive voices that say, "You can do this." During the journey, they introduce you to the eight habits of wise women managing money and give you the tools to continue throughout your lifetime. You will not only begin to enjoy what God has given you in this lifetime, but you will also be prepared to answer with confidence when God asks you in eternity about what you did with what He gave you on earth.

SHARON EPPS
Cofounder, Women Doing Well

This mother-daughter duo combines practical insights, biblical financial principles, and a delightful sense of humor. Whether you are struggling with your first budget, stewarding your investments or planning generous giving, this book will revolutionize your perspective on money and all that God has entrusted to you. If you want to understand why managing your money matters to God—and how to do it wisely—this is the book you need to read.

CHERYL BACHELDER
Former CEO, Popeyes Louisiana Kitchen, Inc.; author, *Dare to Serve: How to Drive Superior Results by Serving Others*

If you are anxious about money, this book is for you. Miriam and Val will guide you through the landscape of spending, saving, investing, and giving, offering wise counsel and practical wisdom, along the way. However daunted you may feel, this biblical, reliable, readable, and enjoyable book will give you the encouragement and confidence you need to manage your money well.

COLIN S. SMITH
Senior Pastor, The Orchard; founder and Bible teacher, Unlocking the Bible

Women are making, marrying, and inheriting money in culture-shaping ways. Fifty-two percent of the wealth in the United States is held by women and only six percent of Christian women surveyed are confident to steward what God is entrusting to them. No matter what season of life you find yourself in, you will want to read *Wise Women Managing Money*. It's practical, relatable, and rich with tools to help guide you into wise money management and increased confidence and courage to live and give in God's image.

JULIE WILSON
President , Women Doing Well

If ever two women are qualified to advise women about managing money wisely, it is Miriam and Valerie. From two generations and two areas of expertise, they give wonderfully practical and—most importantly—biblically based advice that every woman needs. Even if you think you're doing a good job managing your money, you'll discover, as I did, there is room for improvement. Following the wisdom in this book can truly open the door to new financial freedom for you.

MARY WHELCHEL LOWMAN
Founder and Speaker, The Christian Working Woman

Miriam Neff's latest book, *Wise Women Managing Money*, continues to expand her important ministry to women of all generations. Coauthored with her daughter, Valerie Neff Hogan, the book is a good introduction to help women be more confident and understand their money matters. The authors speak from biblical foundations, introducing women to core fundamentals about money and money management. The book's tone is encouraging, and it's written in everyday language—often with a sense of humor. I appreciated the "thinking it over" sections with suggested activities for readers. The "Valerie Says" and "Miriam Says" sections often present personal stories that help to clarify certain money concepts. Their book includes an insightful section on legacy giving, which is often overlooked in other texts about money. That nicely extends typical estate planning information. It's a quick, compelling, and uncomplicated read. I believe this may be a good book for study groups hosted by Christian churches and organizations that want to assist women. Indeed, I wouldn't be surprised to see a short guide prepared for these groups in the future.

KATHLEEN M. REHL, PhD, CFP®, CeFT® EMERITUS
Author, *Moving Forward on Your Own: A Financial Guidebook for Widows*

WI$E WOMEN MANAGING MONEY

EXPERT ADVICE ON DEBT, WEALTH, BUDGETING & MORE

Miriam Neff *and*
Valerie Neff Hogan, JD
CERTIFIED FINANCIAL PLANNER®

MOODY PUBLISHERS
CHICAGO

Edited by Elizabeth Cody Newenhuyse
Cover design: Erik M. Peterson
Interior design: Puckett Smartt
Interior illustrations: Kelsey Fehlberg

ISBN: 978-0-8024-2426-6

Originally delivered by fleets of horse-drawn wagons, the affordable paperbacks from D. L. Moody's publishing house resourced the church and served everyday people. Now, after more than 125 years of publishing and ministry, Moody Publishers' mission remains the same—even if our delivery systems have changed a bit. For more information on other books (and resources) created from a biblical perspective, go to www.moodypublishers.com or write to:

Moody Publishers
820 N. La Salle Boulevard
Chicago, IL 60610

1 3 5 7 9 10 8 6 4 2

Printed in the United States of America

*We dedicate this work to the Lord and to you the reader.
Our goal is to encourage and equip you to step into all of the
excellence and flourishing God has in store for you.*

*We also dedicate this work to the many women who have shared
their financial challenges, wishes, dreams, and realities with us.
We celebrate your hearts to be good stewards of what God has
entrusted to you, and thank you for trusting us with your stories.
That encouraged us to write this book.*

———————————————

The authors' proceeds on this book will go toward
growing women's financial literacy.

CONTENTS

WHAT MATTERS: KNOW IT, OWN IT, LIKE IT, CHANGE IT

Yours, LORD, is the greatness and the power and the glory and the majesty and the splendor, for everything in heaven and earth is yours. Yours, LORD, is the kingdom; you are exalted as head over all.

1 CHRONICLES 29:11

WHY WOULD TWO WOMEN, a mother-daughter team, write a book on money? We are women! Women's perspectives on money are different, as are our resources, the advice we receive, and our reality. Two different perspectives: 1.) vintage counselor, author, single again, widow; and 2.) attorney, Certified Financial Planner, married with children. We are in different life stages and have different investment strategies. Two generations. Some call us a dynamic duo. Actually, we are just highly caffeinated.

We have learned a thing or two in our own seasons of life, not only from our own financial bumps, but from walking beside many women in our ministries and work. We understand the challenges of working together on finances in marriage, and what it's like to go through times of income stagnation. We understand the emotional pull of growing children and young adults—are we launching or enabling them?

Have we not all felt the strong tug of money's strings, tied to our heart instead of our head? We certainly have.

Who should read this book? We have a person in mind as we write. This is likely a woman (but, by all means, guys, you can read this and benefit too). She is an energetic, vibrant woman whom God loves, who feels inadequate or insecure about her finances. She may even feel things are out of control, and she is sick and tired of feeling sick and tired of it. Much like dieting or a new lifestyle of fitness, she is ready for life change in her finances and is finding the landscape of available resources confusing, too complicated, too boring, or not geared to her. But we are ready to see her thrive. To gain confidence, she needs to discover that she can do this. God is with her, and she can win managing money. We will walk this path together and gain strength from each other.

Why do we feel the urgency of addressing money issues today? Consider these facts.

Most women, at some time in their life, will manage their finances and others as well. Women in the United States control 51% of the wealth, and we direct most discretionary spending.[1] Whether ready or not, prepared or unexpected, this is what we do. Over 50% of the women in the United States today are single[2]—solely responsible for their financial affairs.

Women will control two-thirds of private wealth by 2030. Women direct over 70% of spending in the United States.[3]

These facts surprise many women. That reality means we are more influential than we think. Whether we are managing our finances alone, or collaborating with our spouse, our impact is important today. Why is our control of wealth increasing? One reason is that women have different jobs and careers than previously. More women have higher degrees, are employed in higher positions for longer, and with greater income. A second reason is that we are inheriting more wealth. Given our greater longevity, marital wealth and inherited wealth become ours to oversee.

Another fact: Most women lack confidence in the area of finances.[4] We know that all women can master their money and be confident. We also believe that women are values-driven. Each of us has our own personal wishes and values. Even if we are not moving in that direction in our circumstances, we hope to be.

Here is a reality we repeat frequently, without apology: Money is a powerful thing. Direct it or be directed by it. Your money will either go where you tell it to go, or it will take you places you do not want to be.

INVITE GOD INTO THE PROCESS

We will speak from a biblical foundation. God's Word is the best workbook and guideline for finances. His principles apply to those who are wealthy, those with little—even nothing, families, singles, organizations, churches. God is Creator; it is all His, on loan to us. God tells us in 1 Chronicles that everything in heaven and on earth is His. He owns it and loans it to us. We have the privilege and responsibility of stewarding it for His purposes.

What do we mean when we say "steward" or "stewardship"? This is, in a sense, an "old world" word for a manager, or one who manages the belongings of another. In ancient Europe, a steward managed the lord's properties, businesses, and sometimes money. This concept was used all the way back in biblical times as well. There are several passages that speak about stewardship both in the Old Testament and the New. Stewardship is even talked about by Jesus in His parables. The Bible makes it clear that God owns everything, but He has allowed us resources (property, investments, money income) to steward or manage. And He expects us to be wise about it and good at it.

Good money management (stewardship) includes getting wisdom on making income, wisely spending, investing, and saving income, and being generous with others and toward things God cares about. We exist for His glory, and the way we get and use money should reflect that.

> **VALERIE SAYS . . .**
>
> *As a lawyer and Certified Financial Planner, I meet with women and couples. It is important for every woman to know what God has entrusted into her hands for good stewardship, whether she is single or married.*
>
> *We can assure you of two great comforts.*
>
> *First, He has a plan, and it is a good one, and it is not secret. Becoming wise means we learn His principles. We learn and embrace them.*
>
> *Second, you are not alone. You might feel like it—*

> *divorced, widowed, or single, trying to work it out. You may be married and finding managing money bumpy at times. God is in this with you. He sees, knows, and cares.*

MONEY POWER BOOSTER: KNOW YOUR "WHY"

What do we need to do to become wise managing money? We women want to learn, explore, share perspectives. We want to help you direct your money to go where you want it to go, spend it on what YOU value. We will share truths and tools. But first, let's talk about motivation.

What matters to each of us is an important and powerful beginning. Ask yourselves these questions: Would I like to have more to spend on education, experiences, generosity? Would I like to feel less stress about my finances?

Those answers are important. Those desires, our passions, ignite energy and the will to change. How are you doing with your finances to get you to your goals? We want to help you start a plan to get from where you are today to where you want to go.

We lose our way when we lose our why. "What," "where," and "how" become hard things, or just too challenging to achieve if we have lost the vision of "why."

Being more generous to a cause we value motivates us to stay within our spending plan. A commitment to be generous with our church, or other organizations that help others, helps us ignore the temptation to spend. We have included in chapter 9 a rating scale for ranking your values. Focusing on your "why" will highlight what matters to you.

Take a mental snapshot: bank account, bills, credit cards. What does that picture look like?

Do I like it?

Can that get me where I want to go?

Know it, own it, like it, or change it.

HERE ARE THREE THINGS *YOU NEED* TO WISELY MANAGE MONEY

First, the desire to do so. (But necessity is a good motivator as well.) Change will not come because we tell you how to do it. If your heart is not in it, it is not your desire. Your financial habits revert to the same, sooner or later. If it is what someone else values, we will fall back to where we were with no motivation to do the heavy lifting of change.

Values reflect more than money. When we act on our values, we experience less stress, and less debt. This confidence equals more margin, more generosity, margin for a rainy day. You have determined your goals, what's important to you.

This is a sit-down moment to journal. Questions to ponder as you journal:

- The mental snapshot of my bank account shows money going to _____. List the top four categories.

- Is that what I value? Am I on autopay? What is my desire for what I "ought to" pay?

- The mental snapshot of my credit card shows that I value _____. List the top four categories.

- Is that what I value?

- Do I like these pictures?

- Are these habits and trends sustainable?

This journal entry will be a valuable look back in the months ahead!

Second, you need to have the willingness to read and become informed. The fact that you are reading this book means you are willing to learn. You will be doing some new things. Yes, it can be fun! We are not promising that it IS fun, just that it CAN be.

The place where you are took time. Our friend Sue found herself drowning in credit card debt. She works consistently, is single, delightful, and a Christ follower. Thankfully, she hit the pause button and recognized she needed help to reverse this. A dependable debt managing company offered her a workable plan. Her paycheck went to them. She received a portion for her living allowance. They negotiated, worked, and she was debt free in five years. Easy? No! However, she is remaining debt-free, burden-free, and is grateful for success.

Getting to a different place will take time, but it will not happen if we do the same things we did before.

Third, you need basic math skills of adding and subtracting, or a calculator. With simply a fourth-grade mathematics skill level, you can do all this, including managing your investments. We are serious. We will be talking about keeping records, income, what is going out. You need not be an economist. Again, just be willing to add and subtract or use a simple calculator.

THE BIG T: OWN IT—OWE IT

So—the very beginning is where? It is assessing your financial "state of the state." We start with fact-finding. You will need to get very familiar with three ways to track your money.

1. What you own and what you owe.

Sometimes this is called a balance sheet (yikes, technical talk already); or it is collectively called "net worth"—a term we personally hate. We call it "net" and leave off the worth. As believers, our worth is infinitely more than the net dollars we control.

Anywhoo, to track this you draw a large upside-down T on

What We Own	What We Owe
checking and savings accounts	credit cards
home/living space	student loan
IRA, 401(k), 403(b)	mortgage
automobile (its worth)	other loans

a sheet of paper. On one side, list everything you own, major items that have cash value like your bank accounts: checking and savings, your house (its current realistic value), any other accounts (IRA, 401k, 403b), possibly cars, boats, etc., IF you could sell them for that much cash—TODAY.

Now list on the other side what you owe—credit card balances, car loan balances, student loan balances, home mortgage—anything you owe a balance on. Loans you have from family members and friends go here also. We do not list subscriptions here.

Now run the total on both sides and make a grand total. Is it a positive number? Or a negative number? We will call this "net." It is a good idea to revisit this number and sheet at least quarterly—it is a dose of reality. This is not a minimum monthly payment kind of tracking. This is where we track real progress on the big picture. There are many reasons your number could be negative. Maybe you are young, have student debt, are in college, owe on a large mortgage, etc. As you get older, you will need this number to be positive and high. More on that later.

2. A budget.

Yikes—the big bad B word. We are calling it a spending plan. This is a guiding document that will likely take you a year or so to get correct, so do it in pencil. You need to get a handle on all of the categories you spend in, then get an estimate of how much money goes to each of those categories each month. Why? Because you need bowling bumper pads for spending. Everybody does. No one has an infinite amount of money. To control your finances, you need to know what you WANT to spend in each category. Next question, you can do that? Here is an example. Your heating bill. You likely spend something each month. Maybe it is $100 in the winter months, and $50 in the summer months. So budget $75 per month. This way, in the summer, you will build up a balance for those winter months. And—bonus—that bill will not be a surprise, because you know it is coming. It is part of your spending plan.

Your spending plan is rather like bowling. Imagine that bowling ball as your cash. A strike is hitting those spending plan goals. Imagine your cash rolling off into the side gutter. Not having or using a spending plan is where some fall off the ledge or land in the gutter with that bowling ball. They may never come back to master their finances, and that is SO unnecessary. This is not hard, but it takes a little work and perseverance, and you win. Just like a workout.

Why did we say a year? It takes a whole year for most people to cycle through all possible expenses. That twice-a-year car insurance bill, dentist visit bills, Christmas, tax time, etc. We tend to forget about expenses that don't come up every month. We explore this in chapter 3. Remember, we are walking with you.

3. The Tracking Document.

Here is the heavy lifting of controlling what you spend and have. You need to track—somehow—where you are actually spending money. Every expense. This is the only way to familiarize yourself with reality. When starting out, every day, every expense—track it. Online, in an app, on paper, somewhere. Commit to one week at a time, one month.

This is another big place where folks fall off the ledge (or land in the bowling ball gutter, same analogy) toward financial awesomeness. But it is so unnecessary. Want to be extraordinary? Track what you spend. Know where your hard-earned money is going. Most people do not.

THINKING IT OVER

We have offered two sets of tools, three things you need, and three tracking documents to assemble. But looking back at first things first, remember your "why."

Our perspective is simply that money matters for one reason. It is all God's on loan to us. Our greatest desire is to be good stewards. That is our motivation to be wise. To be clear, there are no guarantees that anyone will amass great wealth, but God loves seeing a wise steward. His word says so. He sees our hearts and stands ready to help. And He loves a cheerful giver. (And to be that giver, we need some surplus to give.) So, if you know this lady . . . or are this lady . . . let's go!

TROUBLED TIMES:
CHANGE, CRISIS, OR CHAOS

For the Spirit God gave us does not make us timid,
but gives us power, love, and self-discipline.

2 TIMOTHY 1:7

YOU HAVE STARTED! You are on a mission to be wise with money. You know your "why." You are motivated. You have created your T—what you own and what you owe. You are stepping up to create your own spending plan. You are tracking everything. You have established a solid foundation and are ready to take the next steps.

But life is constantly shifting and you're wondering how to move forward in light of recent events in your world. Life got bumpy and money became a dreaded word. Your focus may even be "How do I just get through this?" Whether this life shift is gentle or cataclysmic, not only has your focus shifted, your financial reality has changed. The change is not in a direction you planned.

Whether job loss, divorce, death of a spouse, foreclosure, or health issues, your paycheck has frozen, or shrunk, but your bills have not. You may not have the time or mental energy to tackle what seems like an overwhelming thing—getting a handle on your money.

That shift might be positive: an inheritance, a job promotion with greater pay and perks, a bonus, or even generosity from an unknown source. Or maybe you are entering the work force for the first time or after a time at home parenting. You have more money!

Regardless of whether the shift brings less money or more, the truth for both is that responsibility goes with the shift, either direction. Can you do it? You can! Change never reverts to past reality no matter how we wish or dream. It is okay to reflect. Bankruptcy, divorce, job loss, health issues, death, or addictions—some of these might have been beyond your control. Yes, some reflection on how we got to the place we are in is worthwhile. Camping out there, immobilized—not a good idea.

You would like a different reality. You may not even know what that is. God is ready to partner with you. He is not shocked. If a past disaster was beyond your control, or if it was not, or maybe you just want to do better, He is ready to help you move on.

You may be pleased with the new reality, but unsure of how to initiate change.

Let's review some foundational truths from Scripture.

God listens and sees your actions. "So then, each of us will give an account of ourselves to God" (Rom. 14:12).

We are not responsible for that other person, organization,

or any other entity. Our task is to commit to planning well where we go from here. "Many are the plans in a person's heart, but it is the LORD's purpose that prevails" (Prov. 19:21). He sees your motivation and stands with you. "Better a little with the fear of the LORD than great wealth with turmoil" (Prov. 15:16).

Change may mean you have less. Or more. The common worldview today is that how much you have defines your value, your reputation, your popularity; therefore, get as much as you can and show it. But God sees you differently. We repeat. He stands with you.

WHAT NOW?

"For the Spirit God gave us does not make us timid, but gives us power, love and self-discipline" (2 Tim. 1:7).

Let's look at how we can walk in "power, love, and self-discipline." We suggest two steps to take.

First, hit the pause button. Do not make any major decisions for a while. Speedy reactions are usually unwise. Intentional actions take you in a new direction. Change is not easy, but required—unless we prefer to remain in chaos and crisis. Folks quickly marry the wrong person to fill a void, sell homes, put down payments on a different living space or a car when their minds are muddy with stress and numbness. Retail therapy, shopping to feel better, rewarding yourself in your sadness, is not therapy. More stuff, even more debt.

Second, take another look at your spending plan. We touched on this in chapter 1; we will dig in further in chapter 3.

The point is that rarely does change *not* impact either what is coming in, or going out, or both. You might find surprises.

It is not unusual after divorce or death to discover your spouse's unrevealed debt. We will talk more about dealing with emotional upheaval in chapter 13. Facing the truth is necessary. "The truth will set you free" (John 8:32). Some changes may be necessary such as giving up an expensive leased car. You may need to get rid of unnecessary costs like cable and smartphones. That comfort coffee drive-thru may need to be on the optional list. Those changes are good. But wait on longer and bigger commitments. Settle your life, your emotions. Breathe.

If more is coming in, avoid the impulse to go on a spending spree. Okay, maybe a super special coffee latte is okay while pondering. First, thank God for the blessing. Then, make a plan —maybe a plan A and a plan B to contemplate moving forward.

HABITS THAT HURT. HABITS THAT HELP.

Most of us are people of habits. When good, they simplify our life. Autopilot for living. Think mundane: brushing your teeth, starting a vehicle. Not all are positive. Consider these two habits that might need to be changed.

1. Inertia

It is tempting to be in cruise control, also called denial. We can keep financial habits that do not take us to our goal. Money is a powerful distraction, even ruler of our soul. Turmoil is draining. Think of the peace you would have if you were actively managing your money instead of cruise control or stagnation. You want to make intentional progress. Please know that even small steps are important.

2. Influencers

Be careful who you are listening to. Some do not have your best interests at heart. They say what they think you want to hear. Buy it, you will feel better. You are lonely, marry again. Every person sees life through their own lens. They likely have an incomplete picture of your changing reality. In the midst of change, we are vulnerable. The advice and input of others matters. God's plan is that we listen to wise people. "Plans fail for lack of counsel, but with many advisers they succeed" (Prov. 15:22). We have a graphic to help.

Imagine in your mind a boardroom—big table, chairs, your boardroom, your board of directors. And you sit at the head. Actually, Christ does. We suggest that you select six people to join you. You listen to the wisdom of their perspective. We call this your Board of Directors.

Facing challenges can be isolating. Even our own thinking can get muddy. These are "advisors" YOU pick. A person cannot invite themselves, land in a chair at your board. You invite each intentionally. We suggest these six:

1. A godly person who has had similar experiences.

"The lips of the righteous nourish many" (Prov. 10:21).

No two people's experiences are exactly alike. We never say, "I understand." But another who has gone through a time of unemployment, or a divorce, or other change can share what was helpful to them. And what was not. Note, we say godly person. This does not mean their faith was not shaken. It means they landed, trusting God.

2. A non-relative wise in finances.

"Honor the LORD with your wealth, with the firstfruits of all your crops" (Prov. 3:9).

"The earth is the LORD's, and everything in it, the world, and all who live in it" (Ps. 24:1).

"Wealth attracts many friends, but even the closest friend of the poor person deserts them" (Prov. 19:4).

This person needs to have a track record of financial stability and not be looking to sell you a product. You need not reveal your financial reality in numbers. But share where you struggle. This person encourages you not to incur debt, or "hand out" to gain favor or friendship. Practical insights right-size our perspective and empower us to make good choices.

Why a non-relative, you might wonder? Relatives are probably already weighing in with their viewpoint. Often they are too close to the situation to be impartial and give objective feedback.

3. A practical friend.

This person knows you well enough to be able to say, "Looks like you're not taking care of yourself. How are you doing?" Or they walk through your living space and see neglect. You trust their friendship enough to let them know how despondent you feel. They might even pitch in to address clutter or gift a wardrobe item that lifts your spirits. Even a plant can lighten our heavy heart.

Common sense is uncommon. And you need such a person sitting at your table. You trust them to listen and make suggestions based on YOUR well-being. You know they are not judging or being critical. They care.

4. An encourager.

"Finally, brothers and sisters, whatever is true, whatever is noble, whatever is right, whatever is pure, whatever is lovely, whatever is admirable—if anything is excellent or praiseworthy—think about such things" (Phil. 4:8).

Complainers should not have a chair at your table. You need people who lift *you* up. Have you been that "uplifter" in many of your relationships? This might be a pause time for that relationship. Maybe again later, but not this season.

5. A person with spiritual discernment and courage.

"As iron sharpens iron, so one person sharpens another" (Prov. 27:17).

This person recognizes if you are allowing yourself to be drawn into a harmful relationship. They help affirm your faith when it's quaking. They recognize enabling, or manipulative behavior in those around you. They have discernment to see, and courage to speak truth. Valuable.

6. A relative whose priority is YOUR well-being.

Family trees shake when change happens. Can we be blunt here? Where money is involved, motivations surface in people we did not know existed before. Yes, even in relatives.

We can discern who is clear-headed and knows the family tree. Their perspective can help us not be swayed while the "tree" is taking its new shape.

One final thought. Remember, you are sitting at the head of the table. Actually, God is, but you are the person. Listen, evaluate, weigh what you have heard and your options. Some of us journal to clarify our thoughts. Final decisions rest with us. We stand before God alone to give account of our actions. Responsibility? Yes. And the sure assurance that He was, is, and will be walking with us.

THINKING IT OVER

We have looked in chapter 1 at our financial reality. Now we have looked at the live "snapshot in time" of our living circumstance today—comfortable and controlled, or in change. In the next chapter, we'll do a deep dive into that spending plan.

A worthwhile follow-up exercise is to sketch your Board of Directors. Write the name of the person you will be listening to for each chair at your table. Throughout reading this book you may be contacting them for feedback, or at least considering what you think they would advise. And remember God's promise: power, love, and self-discipline.

SPENDING PLAN: INCOMING—OUTGOING A MATCH?

Earn money before you spend money.

Put your outdoor work in order and get your fields ready;
after that, build your house.

PROVERBS 24:27

WHO LIKES THE WORD "BUDGET"? We don't. So let's talk about our spending plan. In chapter 1 we talked about a tracking plan. Before we do a deep dive into that, as important as that is, let's start with what is basic. MOST important: work and earn first, and then spend. It is biblical. "Put your outdoor work in order and get your fields ready; after that, build your house" (Prov. 24:27).

Our culture, advertising, and popular trends all pull us in the opposite direction. Their powerful voice calls, "Spend what you want and hope your income will cover it." This is a recipe for disaster. Easy credit, increased debt, financial foolishness, discouragement, even hopelessness.

Upfront fact: The spending plan is subject to and must fit within what is coming in.

How do we start? In creating a spending plan, even that can be daunting. Let's start at the beginning. We have a few analogies for that.

Getting started is like:

- Eating an elephant—just start biting.
- Climbing a huge mountain.
    - Step 1—stop running in the other direction.
    - Step 2—turn around.
    - Step 3—face the mountain.
    - Step 4—start walking.
    - See—you are already four steps in.
- Losing weight—you did not get where you are overnight, and you will not reverse that overnight. Discipline, tracking, sweat, delayed gratification. It is just like that.

Start by assessing your financial "state of the state." Start with fact-finding.

We have six keys to creating a spending plan. However, even before these, pick a way to keep track of this plan. What will work for you?

> **VALERIE SAYS . . .**
>
> *Mom and I are different, but the task is still the same. She is a paper chart and pencil recorder.*
>
> *My husband and I use a spreadsheet and app. Be flexible. Pick a method, use it. Does it work for you? If not, change it.*

> *A great complex method that discourages you from keeping records is not a plan.*

Now we are ready to start.

First step, what is coming in? Your real income, solid base, not fluctuating bonuses or commission. For most of us, it's predictable. One or two simple entries per month. Does your income vary by season? That record is even more important so you can cover expenses in months of lower income. Seeing, knowing, tracking your income is the first and necessary reality check for success.

Second, what am I spending? We have said before, track all your expenses. We do it differently. If paper and pencil work, great.

VALERIE SAYS . . .

My husband and I find that a spreadsheet works well. What works for you? Write it all down and double check against your credit card account, checks, and banking. While credit cards are an easy record, most of us use some cash. Cash spent needs to go in the category it fits. Tips? Eating out? In a family member's handshake with a bill tucked inside? Record it all.

Will you miss some? Not much! Do not become discouraged. Perfection is never achieved. But aiming and missing is better than not aiming at anything. It becomes a fun thing. Our confidence grows when we know our financial reality.

This is the basis for planning and success ahead.

Third, pay your bills promptly. That late fee is money you threw away. It takes the same time and costs less to pay on time rather than late. Organize bills so they are not scattered, forgotten, and lost. One desk drawer, accordion folders? Again, what works for you.

Fourth, keep track of your Big T (chapter 1). How much you have in assets and your liabilities as well. Assets are what you own. Liabilities are what you owe.

It is easy in the rush of daily living to not know what you have. You may have assets you have ignored. A 403(b) through your workplace is an asset, even though you may not access it until later. Liabilities ahead include mortgage or rent, and property taxes. Do you have a loan coming due? Mortgages and car payments are liabilities. Better to know and be prepared.

Automatic bill paying may help with liabilities. That gives you a record of car payments, insurance, rent or mortgage. This step is important because changes may go unnoticed. Seeing that balance moving in a good direction is a motivator. Use auto bill paying as a tool. Watch each amount carefully. For example, if your car insurance rate goes up, unnoticed by you, you might get overdraft charges because you have insufficient funds given that change.

Fifth, it is time to organize all these documents. By now you have noticed that you have lots of documents. Liability stack and assets, bank statements, hopefully 401k reports.

MIRIAM SAYS . . .

Organization is not my strong point. I am a paper person. I have a file cabinet and MANY folders. If I can do it, YOU can. Pick and prepare a place. This actually becomes fun. It is a sense of "I'm on it." "I know where that is." Confidence grows. "I can do this!"

VALERIE SAYS . . .

My husband and I like apps like "You Need A Budget" (YNAB) or Mint to help you give overall categories.

Our sixth key is talk to other wise people about their choices, including appropriate VIPs on your board of directors. You selected these in chapter 2. You do not need to disclose dollar amounts, income, or bills, but listen to what is working for them. Make your own decisions. Remember, it is God's on loan to you. That motivates us to manage wisely. God is trusting us with that income.

We have said before, tell your money where you want it to go, or it will take you places you do not want to go. Now you see where it is going. Does that represent your goals, your desires, what you want in your future?

You have grabbed your spending plan and are ready to make it work for you. Is it realistic? Financial planners have recommended budget percentages. They are interesting and helpful for comparison. Before we look at those, let's remember, it is all

God's on loan to us. We are not giving back to Him. It is His to begin with. These are general recommended percentages. We have chapters on some specifically to help you make choices.

Many say start with 10% for charitable giving as a benchmark. Scripture says, "For where your treasure is, there your heart will be also" (Matt. 6:21).

Ten percent should go into savings.

Now let's look at recommended percentages given that 80% of your income.

Big chunk, 25% or higher: Household expenses. Mortgage, rent, real estate taxes, and upkeep. Do not fall into the "it's the mortgage payment only" trap. Taxes, insurance, and upkeep are housing costs and not incidentals. They are regular, predictable, and necessary. Think every cost in the right category and in the plan.

Transportation: 10% or higher. Do not think car payment. Think payment, insurance, and upkeep.

Health: 5–10% / Insurance: 10% or higher.

Discretionary categories like food, clothing, entertainment, and vacations vary greatly for different incomes.

Every wise woman managing money has an emergency fund. If you do not have one, start. Anything, even $5.00 a week, is a beginning. The recommended amount will cover three to six months of your budget. Just get started. You will get there!

Check the free charts on websites and compare with your spending plan. Remember, it must total less than is coming in. Earn money before you spend money!

Here is a promise. If you follow these biblical guidelines

for managing money, your confidence will grow. More importantly, you are signaling God that you want to be wise in His eyes. He will walk with you. That is what is important!

THINKING IT OVER

Visuals are so helpful. Make your own pie chart. Calculate your total cost for each category. Change it to the percentage of your income. Draw in a piece of the pie that size. (Perfection not required, but try to be close!)

Do you like each pie piece size? What if the total percent is over 100%? Good to know. Vital to know. We'll include here an example of one pie chart. We are not suggesting that these percentages should be yours. It's just an example.

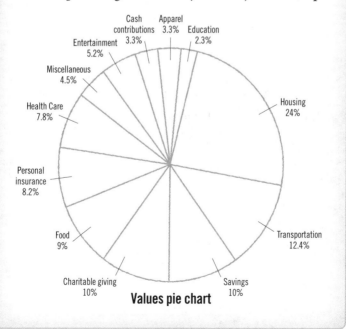

Values pie chart

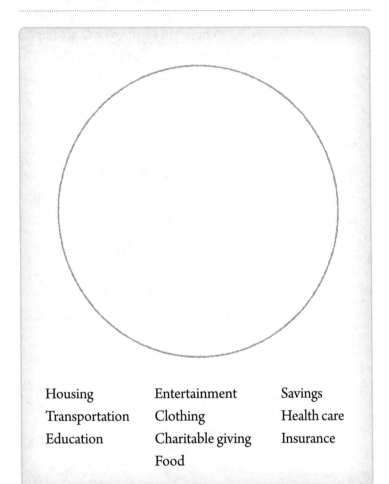

Housing   Entertainment   Savings
Transportation   Clothing   Health care
Education   Charitable giving Insurance
                 Food

CREDIT CARDS

Let no debt remain outstanding,
except the continuing debt to love one another.

ROMANS 13:8

I am not saying this because I am in need,
for I have learned to be content whatever the circumstances.

PHILIPPIANS 4:11

HERE ARE TWO KEY Scriptures relevant to credit cards. The Romans 13:8 verse may be obvious. Credit cards are one of the main ways people end up owing a debt they cannot pay. But the Philippians verse talks about contentment. Problems with contentment often lead to problems with credit cards. So, let's explore the good, the bad, and the ugly about credit cards.

CREDIT CARDS: THE GOOD

Right out of the gate we will say: Every woman needs one card (or line of credit) in her own name to establish a credit score. Some, perhaps many, would disagree with this for various reasons. We will simply say that what we have observed serving women in crisis (who never imagined they would end up in it) for decades now is that women need a line of credit and a credit score. Please disregard this if you are independently wealthy, have housing and income guaranteed for life, a marriage that will never end, and unlimited healthcare provision for life. If you are not sure, let's go on, just in case.

CREDIT HISTORY

What good are credit cards at all? I mean, if you can afford everything you buy outright with cash, why have them?

Often, you will need some line of credit, or more precisely, a credit history/credit record of your own to get an apartment, and sometimes to get a job in certain industries, like banking. You will certainly need that credit history for a mortgage or a business line of credit. There are times when borrowing money is okay, but they are limited.

Having a credit card is also handy for convenience (think: filling a car with gas in January) and to have a record of expenditures. Many credit cards do have the convenience of having a website where you can log in and get spending history, even make a pie chart of the types of spending you have done over the past year. We find that data illustration useful when comparing our spending categories to the values we hold. Ask yourself this question: If I were to make a pie chart of my values, would it match the credit card pie chart of historically spending? Are my "values" and my "actuals" matching up?

Some people would say that getting points or cash back is an added benefit. We do not agree. At best, we think that is a

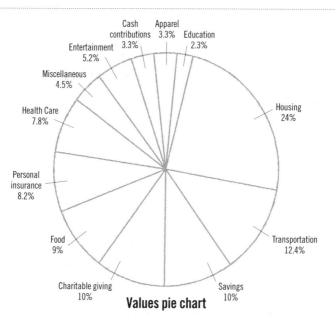

Values pie chart

- Cash contributions 3.3%
- Apparel 3.3%
- Education 2.3%
- Entertainment 5.2%
- Miscellaneous 4.5%
- Health Care 7.8%
- Housing 24%
- Personal insurance 8.2%
- Food 9%
- Transportation 12.4%
- Charitable giving 10%
- Savings 10%

neutral because we tend to spend more with a credit card than we do with using cash. Studies vary that we spend from 12 to 100% more swiping our cards.[1] Cash back programs are simply incentives to spend more. If you see a cash-back program of 100% let us know![2]

CREDIT SCORE

Why does your credit score matter? Lower scores mean you pay higher interest rates on home equity loans, mortgages, vehicle loans, and credit cards.[3] Wouldn't you rather direct that money to what you value? An increasingly important gauge of your financial foundation is your credit report. That report assigns you a number based on whether you pay bills on time, carry debt, have had past bankruptcies. Does that matter?

It does. The lower that score, the higher a mortgage lender

will charge you in interest. Same for credit cards. In fact, a low score may mean that you cannot open a bank account. Then you are left with the currency exchange option for bill paying. Costly. You can get a free yearly credit report at *www.annual creditreport.com*. Check it for accuracy. Remember, resources are all God's on loan to you. Be wise.

Here are reasons you should check your credit score:

1. To know if you indeed did open the account or if someone has fraudulently opened an account in your name. This could be a sign of identity theft.
2. Any old or foreign account should be addressed immediately.
3. Actively close unused accounts. These are fodder for identity theft and credit fraud. They create complexity and have no benefit.

Checking your credit score is time well spent. God has better plans for the resources He has entrusted to you than paying interest.

Have you started watching where your money goes more closely? It is all God's, ours on loan. That is good reason, so spend it carefully and wisely. A low credit score means you are paying high interest.

It is good to understand how your credit score is determined. Here are two factors. The first is payment history: **35 percent of the total credit score** based on making consistent, timely payments. The second is credit utilization: **30 percent of the** total credit score is based on a borrower's credit percentage of available credit versus what has been borrowed.

Your goal should be to make on-time, consistent payments. And use a low amount of the credit available to you.

Most worthy goals are not achieved quickly. Small steps and consistent effort improve your credit score. Your goal: more funds to God-honoring places.

We have talked about payment history and credit utilization. Here are two more factors. Length of credit history: **15 percent of the total credit score** is based on the length of time each account has been open and time since the account's most recent action. New credit and credit mix: **each comprise 10 percent of the total credit score.**

All these factors have nothing to do with wealth. Ten million dollars in the bank will not improve your credit score unless you borrow against it.

CREDIT SCORES: FICO

Credit scores are more important as we use less cash and more credit cards. First, Scripture emphasizes no debt. If you use it, pay it fully each month. Credit scores called FICO range from 300–850.

Understand that your credit score is only a measure of how much debt you have and how faithfully you pay regularly on it. It is not a measure of wealth. It only possibly allows for more access to more credit—in other words, debt. You are entitled to a free credit report. Many sources are listed online.

That report lists all the credit you owe and a status of that account. We encourage you to find out that score and improve it by accountable behavior.

Taking out a new credit card and moving the balance to a lower initial rate, hoping to outrun the calendar? Bad idea. That is why we stress having a budget, a plan, recording realities and change habits.

Remember even small steps are important to redirect what God has entrusted you to His purposes.

CREDIT CARDS: THE BAD

Okay, on to the bad—extreme debt, money wasted on interest payments.

The average American household carries more than $6,200 in credit card debt.[4] We know that the costs take a large chunk out of the income simply to cover interest charges. But there is another great cost.

Carrying debt is more than a financial burden. Hopelessness can set in. "I can't get out from under this." Which may mean, you pay the minimum, it keeps going up, and you feel ever more hopeless.

God never meant for us to live like this. He gave His only Son so we could live free. So why put ourselves in chains?

Meager incomes make it hard to pay bills in full. Penalties accrue. It is a cost of poverty that may seem hopeless. Thankfully, there are some reputable organizations that will come alongside you, consolidate, and sometimes even negotiate lower payoff costs. Yes, they take your paycheck and teach you the disciplines of living within your income. One friend was in that process for five years. Tough learning, but she is now debt-free.

CREDIT CARDS: THE UGLY

The ugly of credit cards—using them can encourage buying what we cannot afford and make us vulnerable to scams.

Being good stewards means we do not reward theft. Credit card fraud continues and we need to be vigilant. We know.

Mom recently spent hours recovering money after being hacked. She had the rude awakening opening her credit card bill. NINE identical charges on one day to an unknown business. Calling the number, they were "closed" that day. We recognized the fraud, and called the credit card company. Scams on credit cards are common. Report that fraudulent charge immediately. Perhaps this has happened to you or someone you know. Fixing it can be a lengthy, difficult process. So how can you protect yourself from fraudsters?

First, use a limited and verified number of companies for orders online. There are companies that are secure and offer great variety. Products available there can be paid through third-party accounts like PayPal. Yes, it takes a bit of time to set that up. However, paying this way could be protection from fraud.

Yes, it is time consuming.

VALERIE SAYS...

Mom's recently canceled card meant she needed to provide the new number to some recurring bills. But taking time to do this is good stewardship—a wise investment. That old credit card number is closed, and she did not need to pay those charges.

Any time you receive an email that appears to be a retailer you use, DO NOT CLICK ON IT. Putting in your credit card number is offering it to scammers and hackers.

Amazon, your bank, utilities, and any other company dealing with finances will not seek your personal information by email. The ploy might be stating that your credit card has been refused and you need to put in a new number. Big mistake. Again, do not click on it.

It is likely we will need to be even more vigilant in the future. Sad to say, fraudsters are savvy. We must be wiser than they are.

There is hope. As we have said earlier, there are organizations to help. As an example, with some companies, a chunk of your income goes to them. They pay regularly, AND they negotiate with credit card companies for forgiveness and lower interest. But fully vet a company before you do this. It is better to get help with discipline than stay in debt.

It is common, given the easy availability of credit cards, to charge to the future what you cannot pay for today. It is tempting to refinance a home and roll that cost in or even secure a home equity loan to pay that credit card. We do not recommend this. First step, go back to your spending plan. How did you build that debt? Pare down spending to increase paying off those cards. To move that debt further jeopardizes your home if you do not get your spending plan in line with your income.

Moving debt from one location to another: not a good idea.

Why resist the temptation to refinance your home and take money to pay off credit cards? Even if the interest is much lower? That action does not change the *habit* of spending more than you earn. Sadly, we see that credit card debt going up again.

Refinancing has costs. Plus, should job loss or other crisis mean you could not pay that mortgage, you are putting your housing at risk. Best plan, revise your spending to pay down credit card debt. As we have said earlier, there are organizations that will help by taking a set amount to pay down debt and negotiate lower costs.

The best plan: owe no one anything but the debt of love, as Romans 13:8 reminds us. Spend only what you have, not what you hope to have in the future.

We love how practical the Bible is. Can you recall a memory where you owed a person money and you could not afford to pay them back? That relationship just gets weird. Maybe it turns into a cycle of avoidance, shame, and discord. This is not how God meant for us to relate to one another. He wants us to "spur one another on toward love and good deeds" (Heb. 10:24), not to duck into another aisle at the grocery store because we owe them $20. Magnify that by 100 when we are talking about those in deep debt with credit collectors.

Contentment to be gained is far greater than any additional thing can bring you. Debt freedom is exactly that: freedom. We are content that God provides all we need.

THINKING IT OVER

Invest some time in examining where you are today and where you wish to be. We suggest these steps:

▶ Know your credit score.

▶ Determine to improve your credit score.

- Best mortgage rates start at a score of 740.

- Good credit scores are 670–850.

- Fair credit scores are 580–669.

- Poor credit scores are 300–579.[5]

▶ Reduce your percentage of available balance use. Using over 10% of your credit card's available balance will lower your credit score.

▶ Never roll one debt onto another.

Contentment to be gained is far greater than any additional "thing" can bring you. Debt freedom is exactly that: freedom. We are content that God provides all we need.

WISE WOMEN:
WHERE TO STORE ASSETS

The man who had received five bags of gold
brought the other five. "Master," he said, "you entrusted me
with five bags of gold. See, I have gained five more."
His master replied, "Well done, good and faithful servant!"

MATTHEW 25:20–21

MORE WOMEN TODAY need to know where to "store" assets
or invest. As we stated earlier (chapter 1), research reveals that
many women feel insecure on this topic. Where should my
assets be? What choices do I have? What matches my needs
and goals? Unapologetically, we advise women to become
wise on financial matters, budgets, and investments. As
women acquire information, knowledge, and understanding, their confidence grows.

Fact: Women today control $70.2 trillion, or 32.5% of
the world's wealth.[1] In the United States, that percent is 51%.[2]
Women control 48% of estates worth more than $5 million.[3]
Women will inherit 70% of the $41 trillion inter-generational

wealth transfer expected over the next 40 years. That's responsibility, and opportunity. Over 50% of women in the United States today are single, never married, divorced, or widowed. God's assets are entrusted to us.

Here is an important distinction. There is a difference between storing and hoarding, stewardship and selfishness. Scripture commends the wise stewards in Matthew 25 whose master gives them money expecting a return. Two doubled that investment and were commended. One did not, and what he had was taken away.

A rich man hoarded his extra grain for himself—bad ending. Joseph stored for the future needs of his people, at God's direction. God blessed. While you will be deciding your need, your wishes and the result of your investments, we trust biblical stewardship and generosity are high priorities.

So let's dig in and start at the beginning. When you are looking to store anything—generally, the reason is you do not need it RIGHT NOW. You will need it LATER. We do not STORE things we need right now. We consume those. But if we immediately consume everything we have, there is nothing stored for when we need it later. This is a fundamental principle with everything we can consume and use: food, clothes, even gasoline in our cars. We gather some things for use right now, and some for later. We heed this principle with food (eat some now, some in the pantry, more gas in the car than we need just to get there so we can get back home). So why is this so often ignored with money?

Statistically, more and more of us are consuming all the

money we bring in right now, even some into the future with credit, without regard to needing some later. And we KNOW we will need money later. We can almost guarantee that!

Let's agree on this established fact: we know we have to set some aside. But where, and for how long? With anything stored away for future use, the big question is: when will you need it? And then: how much will you need? None of us know the future, but this is where some diligent future planning is needed.

SAFE FOR "SOON"

Conventional wisdom and common sense tell us that if you need something soon, do not store it in a risky place. If you lose it, you will not have time to replace it before you need it. This is certainly true with money. So, if you know you will need a certain amount of money in the next year or so, or this money is your emergency fund, you need to store it in a safe place. With money, this means a savings account or a money market account that is FDIC insured.

These are not the funds you will be bragging about at the next cocktail party, celebrating your stock market wins. These are keeping the big bad wolf of credit off your doorstep. Your three to six months' reserves, same concept. Again, these are to keep you fed, clothed, and sleeping indoors if you have no income.

RETURN FOR "LATER"

But what about savings after those two funding needs are met? What if you know you will need to replace a car in three to five years, or if you are saving for a house down payment within the next five years? Or what about for retirement income replacement that may be twenty or forty years down the road?

These are places you may want to branch out and invest funds for return. Time will allow you to take some risk, to get a better return, because you may be able to wait out a down cycle before you need the money.

Another consideration before you invest: what is your risk tolerance?

Will you be able to stomach a market downturn? What if your account loses 25% of its value over a period of time? Are you okay with waiting that out? While that may not be a happy thought, the funds can also increase by 25%, and then compound over time.

Another thought to consider: cost of living generally increases by an average of 2.46% per year over all categories (food, housing, utilities, healthcare, etc.). But if all of your money is "safe" in a savings account making 0.5% interest, you are really *losing* 2% per year. Just to break even, you need to keep up with inflation. Many folks do not consider that about savings and investing.[6]

So, while "safe" low-interest accounts are okay for emergency or income replacement funds, they are typically a bad choice for long-term and retirement funds.

Yet another question you need to answer is: how often do you want to be reviewing and studying your investments? How much time do you have to devote to this? And do you want to devote time to this?

We advocate and seriously admonish you to at least get

to know the basics. If you will spend very little time investing, then you will need a good trustworthy financial planner, and a solid financial plan, and a way to execute that plan and to check up on it at least quarterly.

INVESTMENT OPTIONS

Let's look at the different investment options and their characteristics. Savings account, small return. Bank checking account, none and maybe fees for use. Money market accounts, again small return.

Bonds are buying someone's debt and receiving an interest rate return, sometimes a guaranteed percent return, for a certain time window. You may have heard of short-term bonds, long-term bonds, and intermediate-term bonds. Generally, the longer you loan your money out, the better return you should get. That is how bonds are supposed to work. They are also supposed to be a more stable and more predictable investment than stocks.

Equities, another word for stocks, is ownership in a company. Purchased through a broker or your own account, the historical average return is 9.2% a year.[7] But there's risk. From up years to down years, you need a longer window to ensure you don't have to withdraw your funds on a downturn.

Let's examine another important biblical concept here: DIVERSIFICATION of investments. "Invest in seven ventures, yes, in eight; you do not know what disaster may come upon the land" (Eccl. 11:2).

Picking individual bonds or stocks is long, hard work in

research and can be risky by having too many of your investment eggs (dollars) in one basket. Diversification is the solution to this. What does that mean? Diversification in investments can mean in types of investments: stocks, bonds, money market accounts, mutual and index funds, but also in real estate, gold, timber, and the list goes on. It can also apply to the sector: technology, healthcare, real estate, commodities like oil and copper, etc.

Mutual funds are a basket of all the above, selected by someone else who, you HOPE, will make good choices. You pay the pickers. They are paid whether they make good picks or not. Fees vary from 1/2 percent to much higher and yearly charges. But there are also ETF or Electronically Traded Funds (that means that a computer algorithm chooses when to buy and sell the stocks in that fund, not a human money manager) and Index Funds. Those are generally cheaper in fees because algorithms do not receive salaries and healthcare benefits. These may be good options if you want to diversify and do not have time to research every selection each quarter.

You can check websites like Morningstar to learn how each fund is rated. Funds get graded on how they performed compared to just investing in the overall market or sector that fund is made to compete with. Fund sectors can be categories of companies like technology companies, energy and utility companies, and healthcare companies.

Two very common benchmarks for comparing funds are the S&P 500 and the NASDAQ. Perhaps you have heard about those on the TV, radio, or in publications and wondered what they are.

- The S&P (Standard & Poor's) 500 is an index of 500 large companies in the United States listed on stock exchanges.[8] "The average annual return since its inception in 1926 through 2018 is approximately 10%–11%."[9]

- "The NASDAQ is a US computerized system for trading stocks, especially stocks of high-technology companies."[10]

- The Russell 2000 is an index representing 2,000 small American companies.[11]

We have done a quick overview. We have learned.

VALERIE SAYS . . .

Mom started learning this when Dad went to heaven. And now she loves it!

Women want to learn and we CAN. Being accountable with money and portfolios is a necessity for women as well as men. Eventually we stand before God alone. No finger-pointing, please, as to why we could not, or did not, steward wisely.

Research reveals that even women with high incomes do not feel confident investing. Problem, we become vulnerable to bad advice. Investing requires decision-making, and we can do that. Our investment strategy may be different. Some want stability, some take and tolerate risk for greater growth. Another important point, as we've stated earlier, when are the funds needed?

RESOURCES FOR LEARNING

There are numerous excellent resources that will help you learn investing. Several we like are: Investopedia, Kiplinger's Personal Finance, NerdWallet, Financial Peace, financial newspapers, the *Faith Driven Investor* podcast, and time-tested books like *The Intelligent Investor* by Benjamin Graham—a challenging read. Compare all you learn to the wisdom of God's Word. Many women depend on another person to oversee it all. It is likely every woman will need to do that alone at some time. "95% of women will be their family's primary financial decision maker at some point in their lives."[12]

Learn, pray, get wise council and steward wisely. It is all God's. Invest it wisely for purposes that honor Him.

We like to think of where to store assets like entering a grocery store. Deli section, bakery, paper goods, dairy, and so on. We are entering our investment store. Common sections of our investment grocery store are equities or stocks, mutual funds, bonds, savings and banking accounts, and a shoebox section. We will go into this in depth in chapter 21. Entering our investment store is much more fun than entering a grocery store!

Where do you NOT want to store all assets? In a shoebox: no return. It is God's money and He expects a wise return. We see that in the parable of the talents. It may feel uneasy to branch out into investments. But it is also uneasy to lose money to inflation and to behave like the one talent steward. It was clear that God was unhappy with that one.

We have oversimplified and only scratched the surface here, but hopefully the kickstart helps.

Growing confidence is based on learning, doing, and wisdom from God. If you are blessed with the money to invest, do not bury that talent!

STOCKS: Aisle 5
MUTUAL FUNDS: Aisle 7
BONDS: Aisle 10
SAVINGS ACCOUNTS: Aisle 11
SHOEBOXES: Nope

THINKING IT OVER

Consider making two lists related to investing:

I know about . . .

I want to learn about . . .

We know that growing in our knowledge increases our confidence in overseeing our finances. Consider a trip to your library. We've pictured a stack of our favorite reads in chapter 1. Browse your library's financial section and take those of interest to you.

If you have some investments, take ownership, understand what you have and why resources are parked in the "deli" section they occupy.

Take time, learn, reflect, and pray. Regardless of the size of your "talents" you are entrusted to multiply them.

Pace yourself.

MANAGE IT

HOUSING

*By wisdom a house is built, and through understanding
it is established; through knowledge its rooms are filled
with rare and beautiful treasures.*

PROVERBS 24:3–4

REAL COSTS: OWN OR RENT

OWN OR RENT? Single family or multifamily? How about multi-generational options?

Housing is the single largest expense most of us will incur in our lifetimes. So, much to think about. But let's start, as always, with God's Word.

One of the most important verses in Scripture for wise women managing money is: "Put your outdoor work in order and get your fields ready; after that, build your house" (Prov. 24:27).

The big idea here is to establish your income before you determine where you will live. Much of the Old Testament, in particular, emerged from an agricultural setting. A tiny field—and small income—meant living in a tiny tent or house. The bigger field provided for the possibility of a bigger home.

The principle is true today. We have choices: rent, home ownership, multi-family and multigenerational options.

Home ownership is popular. Typically, a person or couple thinks, how big of a mortgage can I afford? The reality is a home is more than a mortgage. It is upkeep, taxes, utilities, insurance, association fees, and more. Add those on top of that mortgage, those total costs for housing should not be more than 30% of your income. An upkeep budget should be set at minimum of 1% of the home value each year.

In other words, for a $200,000.00 home, every year plan for $2,000.00 for keeping it livable. And that is bare bones. If you ask homeowners how much they spent in home maintenance expenses last year, and they were closely tracking, they would likely cite a higher amount and percentage.

Count on the fact that those other costs will likely go up, not down. That is lots of research and spreadsheet pages before making an offer. If you are married, have LOTS of conversations. How important is that home? What if we value vacations? Will that home mean we cannot get away and escape our routine?

Renting is becoming more popular for several reasons. People change jobs. Life is unpredictable: job loss, health, crisis, divorce. The majority of women in the United States are single. We know that home ownership as a widow has its challenges. In many cities, there is a "break-even percentage calculation" average of five years where you should start to save money in ownership.[1] Researching the area you are considering to buy a home is time well spent. If that location is not break-even in that five-year window, usually rental is recommended. And while choosing is not always 100% budget driven, the numbers should be a primary factor.

Another factor to consider is, how handy are you? Or your close family members? Is fixing up a space a hobby for you? If not, consider that this is a large way homeowners spend their time.

LOCATION IS MORE THAN LIVING SPACE

VALERIE SAYS . . .

For my family, home choices are about more than a living space. We needed to consider walk time to public transportation, school for our children, and proximity to an airport.

I hear young couples say they need to buy a home before they have that first baby. How much room does a baby really need? I am pretty sure I have never seen a newborn baby over two feet long. Will the big home sell when children launch? (Mom tells me they do not launch, they boomerang!)

Here is what is happening in our state. Large homes are selling for less than expected. Small home prices are increasing dramatically. We have a shortage of two- to three-bedroom homes for that first-time buyer or empty nesters wanting to size down.

Be hesitant to increase what you are willing to pay for that smaller home. Consider the numbers for renting. That rental may not be your final destination, but a wise move as prices settle in your state. Also, consider buying something not quite "move-in ready." Move-in ready, no changes required, means you will pay a premium for that home.

In our area, you will also pay a premium for buying in the spring or summer. Consider skipping the premium times and conditions, and go small if possible.

When you have a smaller living space, you will pay less to furnish it, heat or cool it, and less to clean and care for it. Less insurance, less property tax. More to save, spend, and give. We call that freedom.

THINK ABOUT IT

Sometimes we think the Old Testament people had it easier. They lived in tents! When they needed to move, all they had to do was pack it up and go.

Not so today. Selling and buying homes today is complicated. Those transactions cost big money, including Realtor, title fees, appraisals, repairs, and inspections. Nothing is free. Someone pays those, and it is probably you. Those costs may be bundled into your mortgage, but that is not necessarily better. You will pay interest on them, for a long time!

In those tent days, people were not tempted to get home equity loans. Banks want to "HELP" you with those. Let's be clear. You are taking money out of your home equity to pay for something you have not saved for. We know it is tempting: a different car, an expensive home repair, even college costs. Here is a reason not to use them. If you cannot pay that home equity loan amount and the mortgage, you can lose your home! We encourage growing your emergency fund instead of taking a home equity loan. And consider slowly saving for those upgrades. You will appreciate them more and appreciate the freedom of skipping the increased debt load.

IS YOUR HOME AN INVESTMENT?

Back in the day, we thought of homes as an investment. Many of us did benefit from steadily rising home values. That has changed. We are seeing unexpected gyrations in the housing market. New tax laws and limited property tax deductions have changed greatly. Heads up, youngsters (and downsizers, and sandwich generation)! Your home value *can* go down, and that mortgage payment and home equity loan payment stays the same, or goes up, if you have an ARM (adjustable rate mortgage) loan. That is what the mortgage industry affectionately refers to as being "upside down." That is as bad as it sounds. You owe more than your home is worth, if you had to sell it right now.

Reverse mortgages are tempting for vintage persons. Generally, they are not a good idea. You are giving that lender much of your equity. If you want to leave a legacy or inheritance, passing on home value to your heirs can be a tax-advantaged way to leave money to children if done correctly in a trust. A reverse mortgage can counteract that goal. The mortgage company gets that home when you exit this planet.

Better options are planning ahead for days when your income will be less and cost of living will be higher. Plan to retire without a mortgage. Add emergency funds for the unexpected. Which, we can always expect, can't we?

Now, let's talk about the inside of the space and the things we put in it. We have each owned four homes. Upsized, downsized, and midsized. We have done work on each place we have owned, whether we lived in it or rented it out. Like anything else in life, all things in moderation applies here. We love working on homes and putting "sweat equity" in and getting value out. But God has ideas for what we do with our lives other than beautifying our surroundings. Like, ministry.

We can easily to go overboard if we do not have perspective. Certainly, with Pinterest and HGTV, home improvement can become an idol. God meant for us to own and manage our home. He did not intend for it to own and manage us.

> **VALERIE SAYS . . .**
> *Here is some wisdom I have learned over the years. Let someone else buy full-price lovely things. Then I can get them a little later, slightly used. We have three big boys, so even on the rare occasion we did buy brand-new, things did not stay that way for long. In the end, it is all headed to the landfill, and we are headed for heaven.*

So don't let your heart treasure home stuff. Appreciate beauty, but love God and people. Balance, perspective, live your life to glorify Christ. Embrace moderation as your recipe for successful home ownership or renting.

God cares about a sparrow falling, knows the hairs on your head. He clothes the lily. He cares about the space you live in. He cares about that dollar spent wisely. He cares about YOU.

As you make plans, bring them before the Lord. Home is where we spend so much of our time, but is not our eternal destination. If you plan to buy a home, ask God to give you wisdom about how much of His resources He would like for you to put toward His house you will be living in. Remembering it is all His, especially with our homes, puts things into perspective.

SHARING A SPACE

An increasing phenomenon in living space with the sandwich generation and others is multigenerational living. This may be newer for the US, but it is certainly not new worldwide. In other countries, this is the norm, and in biblical times, it was common. As we increasingly have families with two jobs, children at home, and sometimes grandparents needing care, it is likely many at some time will have a multigenerational living space stage.

There are some great advantages. Typically, these include savings on home costs, readily available child and pet sitters, and more help with chores for grandparents. But it is not easy. Our Western culture is based in independence and individualism. Sharing a space with others requires a great deal of compromise and humility. If you must have your own way and preferences most of the time, this is not the path for you. But many make it work. Many of the traits we are admonished to have as Christ followers are the same traits that make for successful multigenerational living. But each should try to be capable of self-support eventually. Choosing this option is much different than having no other option.

One blessing of multigenerational living is getting to know, understand, and appreciate family members in new ways. Meeting friends of grandchildren, meeting their "potential" spouses, glimpsing a bit of the unique creation of each, is a blessing beyond measure. Proverbs 24:3–4 takes on a new meaning: "By wisdom a house is built, and through understanding it is established; through knowledge its rooms are filled with rare and beautiful treasures."

Whether multigenerational, a family of many, or one, beauty is not in the space or the stuff. It is the people.

THINKING IT OVER

Accurately determine what percent of your total spending plan that your living space, housing, is costing. Ask yourself this question: I do/do not like the amount, the percentage of my spending plan being consumed by housing. What immediate small ways can shrink that piece of pie? Big changes might take longer. Peace of mind? Priceless.

CARS

From the strength of an ox come abundant harvests.

PROVERBS 14:4

DOES SCRIPTURE TALK ABOUT CARS? Almost. In biblical times, oxen pulled plows and carts, and donkeys were a travel choice. Scripture said take care of them. These animals were important for work, necessary functions for life. Cars are the oxen and donkeys of today. "Thank you, Lord, for cars!"

Let's remember again an all-important truth. All we have is the Lord's. So we steward it, take care of it, and make wise choices.

We need to get to work. How do we choose transportation that works for us? Like any other "tool" that enables us to get a job done, we choose the right tool for the job, to accomplish our goal. If you want to get a nail into the wall, you choose a hammer. If you want to get from one place to another, a car might be the tool you choose. But the first question is: What are you needing to accomplish? Following this at a distance, what do you *want* to accomplish?

Outlining goals, needs, and then wants is an excellent first step in determining what tool you will choose for transportation.

Thinking about goals: First, you need to get from Point A to Point B. Next, dig deeper: how far is that trip? Is there reliable public transportation? Is it walkable, bikeable, Uber-able? Are you in a city or suburb or rural location? Do you need to haul other people or items where you are going? Think about all of these things in choosing.

You want to choose the smartest option for what you need to do. If you drive fifty miles alone back and forth to work every day in a mild climate hauling nothing, do you need a massive SUV or truck? Probably not. But what if you go short distances and have six children? Do you haul tools and large items for work? If you live in a city, can you use public transportation and rideshare or car rental? Rideshare and car rental may seem expensive to you, but so is year-round car insurance and a parking space in a big city.

For one of Val's sons, in one year, we calculated that he could ride in a limo 180 times to equal a car cost plus insurance. Rideshare was half that price. We were shocked at the premium you pay for a male between the ages of twenty-one and twenty-five for car insurance. And we had three of them in our household! There are options—let's break these down.

THE INS AND OUTS OF CAR COSTS

Cars are a popular choice. Let's talk about purchase price. "New" means when you drive it off the lot, the value goes down. Cars are generally a depreciating asset, meaning the value goes down with age, not up. Buying a used car avoids that, but requires that you do your homework on any specific vehicle you are considering. It is not just mileage and repairs, but what were the problems with that make and model? In fact, even new does not mean safe. Research records, new or used. If you are single and handy with cars, you may be able to take more chances than a parent with newborn twins strapped in the back.

We recommend, if at all possible, pay cash. This means you may have to change your car lust. We look at it this way. If you finance a car, you are lighting a match to the interest you pay.

MIRIAM SAYS . . .

You do not want to see pictures of the cars Bob and I owned as newlyweds. We were college students with hand-me-down cars. I will say no more! I commuted to Northwestern in Evanston in Bob's grandfather's old Buick, a bucket of bolts with slow brakes. But we were grateful for the gift, and I drove slowly with lots of distance between myself and other cars.

As we've already noted, a wise man regards the life of his animal. "The righteous care for the needs of their animals" (Prov. 12:10). Many animals in Bible times were used for work and transportation. Just like oxen needed to be cared for in biblical times, cars require upkeep, repairs, gas, and insurance. That is part of your car costs. If you must borrow, you will probably be offered a low, low monthly amount for five to six years. The car may not last that long! Bad idea. Within a few years, even months you owe more than the vehicle is worth. You can sell the car, get what you can, and still owe money to the lender. Creditors love that plan.

We suggest you delay that purchase and save. Change your car wish for a "reality" car.

Car ownership requires insurance. The more expensive the car, the more costly the insurance. Some cars that have fast engines and sports features may have even costlier insurance compared with a less sporty car that costs the same. Ask your insurance agent what the annual cost to insure that year, make and model is BEFORE you buy it.

Accidents happen. Insurance pays most of it, but you pay the deductible. Let's talk numbers. Crash! You file a claim for $1,000.00. If you have a $200.00 deductible, you pay it. Insurance pays $800.00. Your monthly cost will be lower if you increase your deductible. Have that amount available in your emergency fund. Typically, that saves you money.

Fewer people are choosing to own cars. Especially city dwellers are increasingly choosing public transportation. You can study, sleep, or read. Uber and Lyft might be cheaper than car ownership.

Think about return on investment. If you have an eighteen-year-old son, which will increase value for his future? Car payments or college tuition? You have a twenty-two-year-old daughter starting her first big job. What will give the greater return on investment? Money spent on a car, or money in a Roth IRA in her name? We want to be wise women managing money. Think return on investment.

It is important to think contentment when it comes to cars.

Val, your dad was 6′3″ and commuted to work. His coworker and family had moved in with us temporarily. These two men crowded into his GEO Metro—definitely a "compact" car—to drive thirty-six miles to work. Some folks thought that was funny. Your dad said, "Yes, I laugh all the way to the bank." Contentment in an uncool car rocks.

"I am not saying this because I am in need, for I have learned to be content whatever the circumstances. I know what it is to be in need, and I know what it is to have plenty. I have learned the secret of being content in any and every situation, whether well fed or hungry, whether living in plenty or in want. I can do all this through him who gives me strength" (Phil. 4:11–13).

We have a challenge for you. Be content with what you have and do not have. Do you have a used car? Repairs will likely be cheaper than buying a new one. Does it have a bit of rust? You can learn how to repair with Bondo on YouTube. You can also grievously harm yourself, so be careful. Like smile wrinkles on a contented person's cheeks, rust shows you are on the move.

As you consider what you want in a car, remember that each upgrade will cost money you cannot spend on something else. How much time will you spend in that car? Are there other budget areas that need the funds more? What is your motivation for that upgrade, make or model? Our identity is in Christ, not in what we drive. Interesting how the world repeatedly shouts at us with a different message. It is not wrong to drive a great car that you love. But examine your why. Calculate the cost. Look at your goals, needs, and wants; then choose wisely. Driving a car with rust may be the best budget option for the time being, but it is not a mark of holiness. Contentment and thanksgiving to God for His provision, whatever you have, is a mark of holiness.

Stepping on a train or bus? Read, relax. You have work time instead of driving frustrations. All that you have, time to spend, funds to invest, cars to drive are God's on loan to you. Be a wise woman managing money. Assess the need and plan accordingly, then travel wisely.

THINKING IT OVER

A good follow-up exercise is to calculate the transportation percent of your pie chart. Remember to include the following:

▶ Purchase price

▶ Fuel

▶ Upkeep

▶ Finance charges

Ask yourself this question (we repeat from the housing chapter):

▶ Do I like this/not like this? Does it represent my values?

Keep in mind these suggestions:

▶ Buy used, pay cash if possible

▶ Never, never finance long-term

▶ Insurance: Higher deductible means lower monthly cost

▶ Do I like my return on investment: College tuition or car or other possibilities?

Contentment is being content with what you have and what you DON'T have.

MANAGING DEBT

Do not conform to the pattern of this world, but be transformed by the renewing of your mind. Then you will be able to test and approve what God's will is—his good, pleasing and perfect will.

ROMANS 12:2

YOU MAY HAVE NOTICED by now that we are not mainstream women, go-with-the-flow mother and daughter, follow the crowd, be part of the herd. "Whatever" is not okay. We are pursuing intentional, God-directed, God-honoring goals, even going against the popular flow. Wade into the stream with us. We will walk upstream together.

Let's talk about debt. Caution: we will not be floating downstream comfortably. Remember, we are telling our money where to go, not wondering where it went.

In this chapter, there will be some repetition of what we have said in the chapters on credit cards, housing, and cars. Some of you may have skipped those chapters, being content in those areas. You may have other debts or just want reassurance on your plan. Let's wade in together.

EASY DOWNSTREAM

Debt is popular and accessible—and it can be destructive. We hope to convince you to only incur debt in a few instances. We also hope to help you obliterate debt if you are carrying that heavy burden.

We have said that debt is a greedy beast. Debt gobbles up your money in interest paid to the lender. This beast's partners are anxiety and even fear. Can I ever repay this? My credit score is costing me money. Anxiety rises. At its extreme, repossession and foreclosure bring fear.

Debt is national and personal. In January 2020, our national debt was well over $27 trillion.[1] The average American household carries almost $145,000 dollars in total debt[2] with the median income being just under $69,000.[3] Like we said, debt is popular.

Christ followers are called to be different from our culture. "Do not conform to the pattern of this world, but be transformed by the renewing of your mind" (Rom. 12:2). The pattern of this world is to accumulate debt. Scripture says, "Let no debt remain outstanding, except the continuing debt to love one another" (Rom. 13:8).

The first big decision is to agree with God. Get rid of the greedy beast!

Please know that you can master this issue because God stands ready to help you. Easily? Quickly? No. But possible, and well worth the effort. It is biblical to calculate carefully, and avoid debt if at all possible. Delay and save.

PITFALLS

Get it, then pay for it.

First, avoid debt except for a home mortgage. And then be frugal. What are you earning, what have you saved? Wait, you might be saying, "Most people I know buy much on time, so other debts besides mortgages are good, right?"

Two decades ago, accumulating debt for home mortgages, an automobile, educational costs, and even a business were wise. As we have stated in previous chapters: things change.

Home ownership was once a source of growing worth. No longer. Fluctuations, downturns, and location conditions may make that a poor choice.

Financing that car is tempting. Salespeople offer tempting

low monthly costs, spread out over more months than the car will survive. Education is no longer a guarantee for a job that enables you to pay the debt. Today, student loans are the second greatest debt behind mortgages.

Incurring debt to start a business is more complex and the pros and cons of financing a business start-up (or borrowing for various business needs) are complex and beyond the scope of our discussion here. This, too, is an area where you need the wisdom of experienced, trustworthy experts.

It is tempting when rates on borrowing are low to take on unwise debt. That lower mortgage rate, an ARM (adjustable rate mortgage) that changes later, might be tempting to buy more housing than is wise. Fact: that ARM will likely float up, and up, and up.

Do not count on income rising with the cost of debt. Recent years have hammered some sectors, with many being without jobs for months. Home equity loans are tempting. Floating rates can be devastating, even causing home foreclosure. Optimism is a good thing. But believing you can pay that loan in a short time may not be realistic. You need facts to support that optimism.

Emotional Turmoil

Financial shipwreck can happen simply by letting our emotions lead. Impulse: I owe it to myself—splurge. I am hurting—retail therapy to the rescue. The mall or online shopping—drown that disappointment. Impulse spending creates waste and debt. Impulse investing denies us the wisdom of research.

Pause, breathe. Note that item you think you must have.

Put it on the calendar to consider a month from now. Is it still worth the cost? One of the best protections for allowing emotions to shipwreck your finances is our mundane spending plan. Not flashy, not easy to create, but a guide through times when emotions are tempting us to spend foolishly.

God's promise is that He stands ready to guide you through emotional turmoil. He sees your heart to follow His guidelines. He is steady and He is with you.

Ignoring change

Seasons of life bring changing financial realities. Millennials, mid-twenties to forty, are earning more than most older Americans did at that same age.[4] They tend to collect less stuff, a good thing. Yet they carry more debt.

One in five millennials carrying debt does not expect to pay off that debt in their lifetime. What would you call consuming or taking something you have no way or intention of paying off? Yes, it is called theft.

Millennials are the largest group in the work force, the most self-focused group. It is always a temptation to acquire, using credit for immediate gratification, no matter your age. Other generations, like the two of us, can set good examples in our families, and in our network of friends and acquaintances.

Becoming family shifts more than your access to a good night's sleep. Babies eat, their feet grow, and they bring the unexpected. Special tutoring, athletic gear, and interesting outings. And children notice what others have.

Count on many conversations AND required changes in

your spending plan. Regardless of packed schedules, ignoring the impact on finances of change does NOT change the news. Those regular communication and planning times are rewarded with peace of mind, and unity in marriage.

Risks of debt

Did you know that carrying debt waves a flag to schemers and scammers? Anxious people are vulnerable to "quick fix" plans.

One scheme promises a better rate on a common bill like credit cards, utilities, mortgage rate, or any other bait they can imagine. They target those carrying debt. To "qualify," they require bank and credit card information. Result: your bank is hacked and those bills are the same or higher. Do not open the door or give information in person or by phone. Vet any resource and get wise advice. If it sounds too good to be true, it likely is too good to be true.

Meager incomes make it hard to pay bills in full. Penalties accrue. It is a cost of poverty that may seem hopeless. Thankfully, there are some reputable organizations that will come alongside you, consolidate, and sometimes even negotiate lower payoff costs. We referred earlier to those for credit card consolidation. Some consolidate many debts. Yes, they take your paycheck and teach you the disciplines, yes DISCIPLINES, of living within your income. Some reputable credit consolidation companies are: Credit.org, CuraDebt, and Trinity Debt Management. Vet any organization thoroughly.

What do folks say about them? Will your credit score take a hit? How are they licensed? Research is time well invested.

Sadly, there are predators in impoverished neighborhoods. They knock on doors where they expect folks to be struggling and hungry for solutions to lighten their debt loads. They identify with their predicament and are there to "help." We repeat. Do not answer the door or give out any information.

We talked about credit scores in chapter 4. It is important to mention here again that low credit scores have other costs. When applying for any loan, including a home mortgage, if your credit score is low, you are charged a higher rate.

Some jobs are closed to those with debt. One city refuses licenses to be a barber or beautician, or cab driver due to debt. Some school districts do not hire based on debt and credit score as well.

We hope we have convinced you to tackle debt repayment as a priority. If you are not carrying debt, we applaud you!

SORTING IT OUT

If you are looking at the greedy beast of debt and feel discouraged, remember an important motivator from chapter 1. Know your "why." Remember those areas you value where you would like to have more. Whether education, generosity, experiences, or peace instead of anxiety, let your "why" motivate you.

Answer this question for more motivation. "Who owns our stuff?" Remember the biblical view of ownership. It is all His, on loan to us. Not 10 percent His as a donation and 90 percent ours. It is 100 percent His for us to steward wisely.

Conformity to subtle debt accumulation is easy. Transformation? Not so much. Prayer, discernment, replacing self-motivation with God motivation—these start the process.

Consider this for additional motivation. "Since we are surrounded by such a great cloud of witnesses, let us throw off everything that hinders and the sin that so easily entangles. And let us run with perseverance the race marked out for us" (Heb. 12:1). Scripture compares life to a race to be run well.

What race has the Lord asked you to run? Are you weighed down by unnecessary things? How much time/energy does it take to manage, insure, dust, store your stuff? Picture a donkey pulling a cart that is tipping him backward, overloaded with stuff. Contrast a lean, fast runner on the move. God usually allows you to choose to lay aside weighty stuff. Rarely does He remove them Himself.

You can be debt-free. It is your choice. God sees your heart. You are not running alone. He is running with you.

Remember, it is your heart He cares most about.

THINKING IT OVER

Look back over the T you created in chapter 1. You have a list there of what you owe. Is it complete? Calculate your total debt.

Next question: My debt elimination goal is_____ by _____. Just start! As we've said before, you have the peace of beginning, and you've signaled to God that you agree with Him about debt.

Another worthwhile thought to consider is this: _____tempts me to overspend. We've said so often: Know It, Own It, Like It, Change It. Even baby steps of change are gratifying.

9

DISCRETIONARY: CLOTHES, FOOD, ENTERTAINMENT

I am not saying this because I am in need, for I have learned to be **content** *whatever the circumstances.*

PHILIPPIANS 4:11

I know what it is to be in need, and I know what it is to have plenty. I have learned the secret of being **content** *in any and every situation, whether well fed or hungry, whether living in plenty or in want.*

PHILIPPIANS 4:12

But godliness with **contentment** *is great gain.*

1 TIMOTHY 6:6

But if we have food and clothing, we will be **content** *with that.*

1 TIMOTHY 6:8

MANAGING OUR SPENDING PLAN is not a one-time task, or a one-size-fits-all effort. Yes, "effort" is a good word. It is not unusual for segments to morph, grow, and either crowd out another item, or be the source of debt.

By now, you know debt is NOT a good idea. When your spending plan is spilling out beyond income, a quick and first look can be at discretionary spending.

DISCRETIONARY	NON-DISCRETIONARY
Clothing, fancy design	Clothing
Fast food	Taxes
Entertainment	Transportation for work and essentials
Hobbies	Utilities
Travel	Housing
Gifts	

Defining terms helps. Spending plans usually are divided into non-discretionary and discretionary spending. Typically, housing, taxes, transportation for work and essentials, and utilities are examples of non-discretionary spending. They are required for living. Yes, you can shrink or grow them. But not easily or quickly. We have talked about housing and transportation in earlier chapters.

Discretionary spending is for things that are not a "must." For many, this category might include designer clothing, fast food/eating out, entertainment, hobbies, travel for leisure, gifts and more. Yes, there is some level of minimal requirements for some of these things, but not all. Wants can morph into "I need that." Our spending plan becomes a spending pit.

Example: We are in Chicago. You cannot turn off the heat in January and survive. But you can eat oatmeal instead of ribeye steaks. Clothing is necessary. But the shopping stop can be at a resale shop or high-end designer shop, either brick-and-mortar or online.

IT IS ALL HIS

Before we dig deeper into details, let's remember our "why." First, remember our perspective. All we have belongs to God, and it is on loan to us to use. That means we spend in ways to honor Him so we can be generous with others and kingdom purposes. What can God do when we put every part of our spending in His hands?

In Matthew 14, Jesus was teaching a large crowd and they got hungry. He asked His disciples what food they could find to feed the crowd. Answer: five loaves of bread and a few fish. Jesus took those, blessed them, and fed probably 20,000 people! He can do amazing things with those chunks in your budget beyond what you can imagine. After that picnic, the disciples collected seven baskets full of leftover bread.

We are not saying that if you put one loaf of bread in your cupboard and open the door there will be twelve loaves there. Or that your two work outfits will be multiplied to twelve. What we are saying is that when you acknowledge it is His, and you are committed to using it for His ways, He works in ways that only He can provide.

DO NOT COMPARE

Another important point is, "No comparisons please." It is easy to look at others, their clothes, living style, and make assumptions, judge, or even try to match appearances. Very bad idea. God has created us all so very differently. He has called us and given us assignments and resources uniquely for us. Let's stay focused on our own spending plan and discretionary expenses.

We have talked about suggested percentages for budget categories in chapter 3. Keep in mind, these are general. You, in your circumstance, may modify that.

We have acknowledged that we women make 80% of all consumer purchases, goods and services.[1] "95% of women will be their family's primary financial decision maker at some point in their lives."[2] We do this, so let's do it wisely.

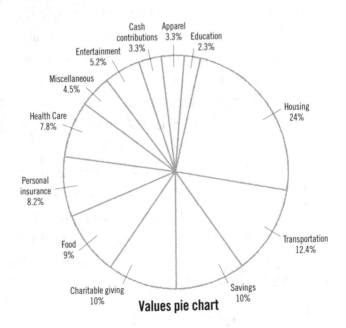

Values pie chart

Let's look again at the suggested percentages for different categories.

Food: 15% max. Personal, including clothing 15% or less, recreation 5%. We can make quick changes in these. Non-discretionary budget items, housing, transportation, and insurance might be set. We cannot make quick changes there.

Shrinking the food budget is hard. Val gets it. She has three grown sons now. They were all super three-sport athletes. That is a lot of food. Two tips: First, plan. She makes that list: for her family, three dozen eggs a week. You make your list. What do you need, enough, not too much? If the fridge is empty, eating out is tempting, even ordering in. But it is a big budget-buster.

Second, go to the store with your list and no charge cards, just cash. When you have cash, you notice that price. Funny how sharp a consumer and mathematician we become when we have a limited amount of cash and do not want to be embarrassed or have to leave items behind at checkout.

Let's talk clothing and personal purchases. Our careers were and are quite different. For a counselor in public high schools, business casual was fine and inexpensive, and variety was not important. As a lawyer, the budget for clothing will be higher. Think about not spending on clothing for six months. You can do it unless you have rapidly growing children. We do clothing swaps. Donate what you are not wearing. That is helpful for another family's spending plan.

Before you buy household, personal, or just fun things, think of using it, dusting it, insuring it, hauling it, storing it. Is the item a need or want? It is okay to purchase an occasional "want," but we challenge you to put it on a wish list and see if it is at the top of the list in one month. You would be surprised.

As we look back at the pandemic of 2020–21 we can underscore a few truths:

- Wise planning does not guarantee all will be smooth, but is certainly better than if we had entered without reserves and a good plan.

- We are flexible when we need to be. Much travel was impossible during the worst of the pandemic. Staycations, not vacations. Home cooking, fun or not, a necessity. Restaurants closed. Zoom wardrobes: business casual shirts and jackets—and sweatpants.

- Employment is a fragile gift. Company loyalty is rare. Proven productivity is helpful.

- Needed skill sets for employment may require retraining, and different certifications. Flexibility to retrain was desirable before, now it is vital.

While 2020 highlighted these realities, they are good facts to remember. Much of our future is unknown. Here are more truths we can depend on.

Contentment comes with your spending plan well within your income.

Spending down, reserves in place, means financial anxiety is also down.

God-blessed priorities, and prayer, mean greater contentment and trust in God.

Let's circle back to remembering our "why." The apostle

Paul wrote these words from a prison cell. "I am not saying this because I am in need, for I have learned to be **content** whatever the circumstances. I know what it is to be in need, and I know what it is to have plenty. I have learned the secret of being **content** in any and every situation, whether well fed or hungry, whether living in plenty or in want" (Phil. 4:11–12).

It is highly unlikely that any of us will ever experience his circumstance. Paul had walked miles through countries, breathing freely outside air. He had been hosted in homes by friends, fed, and housed. Yet he was content in a prison cell. Likely hungry, stale air, even stench, and change unlikely. What can we learn from Paul? Quantity is not comfort. Abundance is not a prerequisite for contentment. External does not define our contentment.

Much of what we own and even depend on was not invented a few decades ago: computers, microwaves, and very smart phones. Closet sizes were once small, no need for a shoe rack. It is not wrong to own these things. Just good to think about and gain perspective when we are creating a God-blessed spending plan.

Our family remembers hiking in the Masai Mara in Kenya, being led by a Masai warrior in full dress. On his feet he wore flip-flops unlike any we had ever seen. He had made them from trashed truck tires discarded on hot roadways. He told us that pair would last his lifetime.

We brought a pair home to remember frugality and adaptability. They are quite comfortable. We own stilettos, crocs, tennis shoes and more. Our professional demands are different. We all need to walk. We wear different shoes, shoes that fit not just our feet, but our spending plan.

THINKING IT OVER

You have made choices. Trimmed some pieces of your pie, maybe even eliminated some. Here is an additional exercise you may find helpful. We are including a Rating Your Life Values chart. The directions are simple. You are prioritizing what you value most. Take time to read, ponder, and rate these sixteen items. You will eventually have your top five.

Compare those to your pie chart and your values pie chart. Do your spending portions reflect your values? While this exercise takes time, we have found it quite motivational in changing percentages in our spending plan, both discretionary and non-discretionary.

RATING YOUR LIFE VALUES

This exercise will help you think about what you value most in your life. Here are sixteen key values that people often say they want to experience. Some say they want more of these values than others. You cannot realize them all because one may contradict another.

Assume you have to give up eleven of these values. Which would they be? Remove them by putting an "X" in the left column. Finally, rank your top five remaining value preferences, from highest (1) to lowest (5).

Achievement	Accomplish something important in life; be involved in significant activities; succeed at what I am doing.
Adventure	Experience variety and excitement; respond to challenging opportunities.
Aesthetics	Appreciate and enjoy beauty for beauty's sake; be artistically creative.
Authority/Power	Be a key decision-maker, directing priorities, activities of others, and/or use of resources.
Autonomy	Be independent, have freedom, live where I want to be and do what I want to do.
Generosity	Give time and/or money to benefit others; express gratitude for blessings in life.
Health	Be physically, mentally, and emotionally well; feel energetic and have a sense of well-being.
Integrity	Be honest and straightforward, just and fair.
Intimacy/ Friendship/Love	Have close personal relationships, experience affection, share life with family and friends.
Pleasure	Experience enjoyment and personal satisfaction from my activities.
Recognition	Be seen as successful; receive acknowledgment for achievements.
Security	Feel stable and comfortable with few changes or anxieties in my life.
Service	Contribute to the quality of other people's lives and help to improve society or the world.
Spiritual Growth	Have communication or harmony with the infinite source of life.
Wealth	Acquire an abundance of money or material possessions; be financially rich.
Wisdom	Have insight, pursue new knowledge, have clear judgment, and use common sense in life situations.
_____ (specify)	

Note: Thanks to Kathleen M. Rehl for her kind permission to adapt this exercise from her "Rating Your Life Values" exercise first published in her book *Moving Forward on Your Own*.

Put your money where your values are. Money can be a means to an end, not just the end itself. When you use your money in ways that reflect your true values, you will probably feel happier, too.

▶ Describe a time when you felt good about spending money in a way that matched your values.

_____

_____

_____

▶ Have you ever spent money in a way that did not support your values? If so, describe that incident.

_____

_____

_____

▶ Look at your number-one top value. What's one way you can use some of your money to align with this important value?

_____

_____

_____

This is a good time to remember: just as creating your spending plan is not a one-size-fits-all exercise, neither is how you divide your pie. This is a good time to remember.

What are my top three values? Does my spending fit in with these?

Know it, Own it, Like it, or Change it

INSURANCE

*Trust in the Lord with all your heart, and lean not
on your own understanding; in all your ways submit to him,
and he will make your paths straight.*

PROVERBS 3:5, 6

> Understanding the role of insurance is a basic
> building block of wise financial stewardship.

MANY TIMES IN THE CHRISTIAN LIFE, we hear references to how we live a "faith walk." We interpret that as meaning that we have to make day-to-day decisions without audible guidance from the Lord, but with a balance of interpreting His Word in the Bible. We are trusting Him for guidance, safety, and provision, and then making wise choices and doing our own due diligence. Understanding the role insurance should play and when you need it is a basic building block of wise financial stewardship. We know we need a work ethic, source of income, a budget to monitor and control that income, and savings for the future "knowns" and "unknowns."

So, let's tackle insurance. Wise women managing money need to know about it, and in many cases have it. Not exciting, not sparkly, but a diligent use of funds to keep the wolf of poverty from any of our doorsteps. We get highly caffeinated to tackle this.

MIRIAM SAYS . . .

I would rather talk investments, but those may not be helpful if you lose your income stream, so let's make this fun!

VALERIE SAYS . . .

That is a stretch, Mom. You like numbers and not spending any money on things you do not need or want. I am a lawyer. I like due diligence and do not like to see people getting sued. That is why we are going to have fun talking about insurance.

Definition: A company or agency provides a guarantee for specific loss in return for paying a premium.

What is it? A company or agency provides a guarantee for specific loss in return for paying a premium. It is a protection against something that might happen or will happen. Many of us could withstand a temporary setback or unexpected cost, especially if we practice wise stewardship with saving. But what about a catastrophic, unexpected loss or expense? Few have so much saved that they can "self-insure" or cover such a loss with their own funds.

What do we mean when we say catastrophic? Here are some examples: getting cancer that continues to come back while having no health insurance, living with dementia for fifteen years with no long-term care insurance, being in a car accident where someone dies and it is determined that you are at fault. Few people sit around and imagine the worst that can happen, and we cannot stave off every misfortune in our lives. We have to trust the Lord with our future, but that does not mean being ill-prepared.

One of the most important, preventable, and heartbreaking things we see are widows without life insurance, especially widows with several young children. Term life insurance is relatively cheap, available through many employers, and can be the difference between a young family making it after a tragic death or becoming financially destitute almost immediately. In so many cases, this is just unnecessary. We could have an entire chapter of testimonials from widows or family left behind where term life insurance would have made a huge difference. Many times, for the yearly coffee budget, that insurance could have been covered that whole year.

Most of us have some type of insurance—life, car, home, health. We need to look at what we have regularly and ask: Does this do what I want it to do? Does this cover what I need? If not, I need to go insurance shopping.

Let's talk *car insurance*. We discussed cars and the need for transportation in chapter 7. Let's dig deeper into the insurance aspect. The more expensive the car, the more complex the repairs, the higher your premium will be. How can you reduce that premium? Increase your deductible, what you pay out of pocket for that fender-bender before the insurance company steps in. That higher deductible will probably save you money IF you keep an emergency fund that can cover that cost. Having adequate LIABILITY insurance as a part of your car insurance is critical.

We live in an increasingly litigious society, and unfortunately, many unethical people think being in a car accident is an opportunity to get rich. Even a legitimate claim for someone in your car who was seriously injured can be devastatingly expensive, especially if they sustain long-term injuries.

Home insurance helps keep us from catastrophic loss that our budget or reserves could not handle. It keeps us away from financial crisis that could otherwise make us bankrupt. Water backup, fire, hailstorm—it is important to adequately insure, but not waste by over-insuring. Again, LIABILITY insurance that can be paired with your homeowners and car insurance is critical. If someone injures themselves or dies in your car or on your property, this can be financially devastating, and liability insurance as an add-on is relatively cheap. It is certainly cheaper than losing all of your assets if there is a wrongful death or negligent act.

Okay, girls, check, compare, and be ready to move to another insurer. Remember, the insurance company is not necessarily loyal to you. They are in business to make a profit. There are people who specialize in comparing for you. Fun times comparing? Not really. But valuable money saved.

It is easy with automatic deduct bills for increases to go unnoticed.

MIRIAM SAYS . . .

This year, my insurance (home and car) went up 10%, even though I filed no claims last year. I called. They said it was the best they could do. I did check with another insurer and read the fine print. My present policy was best.

Important here is KNOW WHAT YOU ARE GETTING. Cheaper is not better if it covers less.

If you are blessed to own your own home, and are hospitable, we recommend an umbrella policy. It is a type of insurance that provides liability coverage over and above your automobile or homeowners insurance policy. For example, if someone is seriously injured on your property or related to your vehicle, their costs might be more than your insurance provides. They might sue for much more. This type of insurance addresses liability.

As we have stated, and it bears repeating, our litigious culture makes this an even more important policy to have. We recommend it.

One wise financial purchase is life insurance. It is easy to decide to get it, challenging to choose which is best for you. Guideline: Decide what life insurance needs to accomplish for you in this season of life and later. In addition to covering costs of celebrations of life and burial, financial provisions lessen the likelihood of poverty for young families and widows. Women typically live longer than men. In eight of ten marriages, men leave this planet before their wives.[1] An act of love is to have adequate life insurance for your spouse.

We see young couples that have no life insurance, even couples with children. Some jobs may provide some, usually not enough. It is a hard discussion, but necessary.

How do you choose an adequate amount of coverage? Choose in proportion to the value you bring to the family. What would it cost to replace Dad's income? Mom's income? Or to hire the tasks she does for the family? Some wish to provide to pay off an existing mortgage. In addition to wise financial stewardship, peace of mind is a great reward.

Let's simplify choices. Whole life is a contract where you pay regular amounts over a prescribed limited period of time for coverage for a lifetime. Death means that amount is paid to beneficiaries. Term means payments and coverage for a limited time. Benefits are only paid if death occurs in that period. Term is much cheaper than whole life.

Beware of considering life insurance a savings plan. The costs usually do not support that. Typically, a combination of term insurance and money saved and invested wisely is the most economical provision for those you love.

Health care costs are rising.

MIRIAM SAYS . . .

My health insurance costs this last year doubled. Here is one bright spot. Many plans have moved to giving an annual account allowance. Those funds can be used for insurance premiums and medical costs not covered by insurance. Why is that positive?

> *It requires that we make choices about our health because the impact on our wallet is direct. We carefully choose plans that meet our needs. We pay attention to preventative lifestyles to avoid health risks, and make choices about treatment more carefully. For example, generic medications may work.*

Telemedicine is becoming a popular option for medical help. Telemedicine offers basic health care through virtual visits with a doctor by phone or video chat. This may be ideal for minor concerns, colds, infections, stomachache, and more. Costs are usually $50.00 compared to $80.00 for an office visit and $125.00 for an urgent care facility visit. Comparing that cost to full costs before your deductible might be a good option for you.

Just as insurance costs are rising, medical costs are as well. This means we need to research, compare, and discover ways to maximize our dollars for medical costs.

We remember Dad's favorite verse: "Trust in the Lord with all your heart and lean not on your own understanding; in all your ways submit to him, and he will make your paths straight" (Prov. 3:5, 6).

Becoming wise women managing money is a strategic balance. Yes, we choose and learn about insurance and everything, but our trust is in the Lord. We do not know whether or when that unknown car crash, sewer back up, or health diagnosis will come. We prepare as best we can. But our complete trust is in God.

THINKING IT OVER

What are all your insurance costs? Make a list. Now you're ready to research. Shop another insurance company for rates for what you have. Remember, compare apples to apples. Is the coverage the same? Same price? Lower? Higher? Most are eager to give you a quote.

Compare all to determine what is best for you, both quality and price.

These will change periodically, usually moving higher. Remember your loyalty is to God as His steward. Pay attention and act, remembering your "why."

LOANING MONEY, COSIGNING CONTRACTS

The LORD will open the heavens, the storehouse of his bounty,
to send rain on your land in season and to bless all the work of your
hands. You will lend to many nations but will borrow from none.

DEUTERONOMY 28:12

> If you usually have a bit of change in your pocket,
> someone will notice, and want it. You will likely be
> asked to loan someone money.

CONGRATULATIONS! You have leaned into following biblical principles on managing money God has entrusted to you. You have a plan to provide for yourself and your family, be generous, and store wisely.

Very likely, someone has noticed and will ask for help. If this has not happened, and you know no friends or family who have been asked for help, just wait. Rarely is that "ask" not a reality.

Sixty percent of Americans have helped out a friend or

family member by lending cash, while 17% have lent their credit card and 21% have cosigned for a financial product. For one-third, the result was a negative experience "resulting in lost money, a damaged credit score or harmed relationship."[1]

While Scripture says we can help those in distress, there is much at stake. Our means are not *our* means. Our ability is based on God entrusting us with His means. Wisdom is required, not just for financial stewardship, but for relationships as well.

Our ever-ready, always excellent source of wisdom and direction—Scripture—addresses this important topic. In this chapter, we will address four important guidelines, as well as wise alternative ideas.

1. You may help those in need without charging interest.

When we are blessed with money, God says loan it, with guidelines. First help those in your family, other believers, the poor without **over** charging interest, even no interest. Do not take advantage of a person in a hard place. "Good will come to those who are generous and lend freely, who conduct their affairs with justice" (Ps. 112:5).

You may lend without charging interest. "If you lend money to one of my people among you who is needy, do not treat it like a business deal; charge no interest" (Ex. 22:25).

It is wrong to borrow without the intent of repaying the loan. "The wicked borrow and do not repay, but the righteous give generously" (Ps. 37:21).

Sadly, some who are in financial difficulties, and are planning to declare bankruptcy, have run up more credit card debt, securing for themselves what they could not afford, knowing they would never repay that debt. Scripture describes this person as "wicked." Strong words.

It is only wise to consider the possibility that the loan will not be paid back. "Could I light a match to that check?" You might never see that loan repaid. Just being real here. Face that reality, most lend with the expectation that the loan will be repaid. Statistically there is a 50% possibility that it will end poorly. Of those who had loaned to a family member and not been repaid, the relationship was damaged.

Just as we are told that we can loan money to those in need, the recipient is responsible to keep their commitment to repay the loan.

2. You may ask for a pledge, surety, of something of value.

Simply defined, this is ensuring that the loan be repaid by holding something of value of the borrowers. Common business examples are car titles or home titles until the loans are paid back. We have said it is okay to loan to the needy without exorbitant interest. It is also okay if to hold something of value as a pledge. Deuteronomy 24:10–13 describes this. While the example is a cloak of value in Old Testament times, the principle applies today. What you hold as a pledge should not result in undue suffering on the part of the borrower.

Our reality today is that many personal loans are to family or friends with nothing held to secure their repayment.[2] An important question to ask is this: "Am I okay if that loan is never paid back?" We know of many, especially widows, who have loaned money to family members and were never paid back.

President Abraham Lincoln was asked for money and saw the difficulty. He proposed that the person go to work "tooth and nail." That is a vintage statement. Lincoln said if he gave him the $80 that person would be back in debt. The requester had a poor work ethic. While you can hold something of value until the loan is repaid, few do. This reality means it is important to consider our next guideline.

3. You may loan to family members or friends only after considering biblical guidelines that are wise and beneficial, not harmful, to that family member or friend.

We know it is hard. Mama's heartstrings. Dad's desires to see success. Family ties have great potential for financial blind spots, giving with emotional strings attached, even giving to compensate for past mistakes. We will not sugarcoat the difficulties. Let's lay out several reasons to just say no.

- *Provide for your family (do not spoil them).*

The Bible has rough words about those that do not provide for their family. "Anyone who does not provide for their relatives, and especially for their own household, has denied the faith and is worse than an unbeliever" (1 Tim. 5:8).

We need to discern when our family members need help, and when they simply want something they cannot acquire for themselves. We have been clear with our children that when they are moving forward doing positive, God-honoring things, we will help give their efforts "rocket boosters." But if they are making decisions and taking actions that tear down the walls of their own life or lives of others, we will not help move even one brick. There is a difference between providing enough and spoiling, or providing too much.

> "Keep falsehood and lies far from me;
> give me neither poverty nor riches,
>   but give me only my daily bread.
> Otherwise, I may have too much and disown you
>   and say, 'Who is the LORD?'
> Or I may become poor and steal,
> and so dishonor the name of my God." (Prov. 30:8–9)

Daily bread is not a new car, or even a dependable used car. It might be public transportation tickets, or a bicycle. Just sayin'.

Daily bread is not the down payment on a home beyond what that friend or family member can afford. It might be agreeing to match savings for a down payment, with a specific ceiling on that amount.

- *Do not help and support foolish behavior (enable).*

Actions have consequences. We all make mistakes and make foolish decisions at times. When we care about someone, we may wish to step between the person and the consequence of what they have done. Maybe this time will be the new start. Enabling is not protecting them. Our intervention ensures that they may repeat the unwise, even illegal behavior without learning a necessary lesson.

Sharon, upon becoming a widow, had a paid-for home and her work income was adequate to cover her living costs. Her adult son had a history of poor financial decisions. After his dad's death, he asked Mom to put the home title in his name as well. We can only guess his intent for this request.

Caring friends in her support group advised her not to do so. Wise counsel. If she would have done that, he could then take out a home equity loan. He had promised her he would pay those loan costs. However, he was not consistently employed. If he defaulted on payments, those would be Sharon's responsibility as well. Her income was inadequate to do so. The lender could foreclose on the home—what had been *her* home. Sharon wisely followed her friends' counsel. She did not enable her son's poor financial behavior.

Widows are especially vulnerable to financial asks from their children. Being lonely, wanting more contact, giving a handout might seem like a way to keep them close. A loving answer is no. If that person, child or friend, cares for you, and has your best interest at heart, they accept "no" with grace.

Remember the guiding principle of Scripture. Earn first

and then spend within that provision. Some "asks" are the result of poor work habits, or simply not living within one's income. Scripture is clear. Do not feed those who will not work. "The one who is unwilling to work shall not eat" (2 Thess. 3:10).

4. Never cosign a loan.

Have you been taught "never say never"? We have a "never" for you and we mean it. Never cosign a loan. You cannot, repeat, can NOT get out of it. Even by dying.

Why is that person asking for a cosigner? Because lenders have determined the person is a poor risk, a risk they will not take. So why are *you* willing to take the risk?

Would you be willing to give that person that amount as a gift? Probably not. Whether a car or even cosigning on an apartment, how accountable are they?

Not cosigning means that individual must face their reality. They have to save for a down payment, or purchase a lesser used car. Or they will need to look for a home or rent an apartment based on their resources. Life lessons for sure. If you have cosigned and they fall behind on payments, your credit score could be damaged.

And one final thought. Here is a scary, but important, topic—over-indulgent grandparents. It is best, but not always easy, to respect the role of parents in training their children. Just like too many chocolate chip cookies, more is not necessarily better.

Communicate, communicate, communicate. We both value education and meaningful travel including world experiences, not fancy new cars. What we provide for them as parents or grandparents shows what we value.

GOOD GIVING IDEAS

We hope to have stimulated your thinking on helpful, not harmful giving. For instance, offer to match (with a limit) a goal that meets your values, and does not enable that person's poor habits. Scripture often refers to accumulating "little by little." An additional benefit is that the person will learn to value and care for that item acquired.

> Roth IRA: an individual retirement account allowing a person to set aside after-tax income up to a specified amount each year. Both earnings on the account and withdrawals after age 59½ are tax-free.

Think about encouraging a child or grandchild to start a Roth IRA, and you can help them fund it. Be careful of having an expected return. Money may not buy you frequent texts from college students, but that Roth IRA will give you a common bond for conversation. There are rules and limits that may change. A simplified description is that a parent or grandparent can open with that person a Roth IRA and fund into that vehicle a specified amount each year. Restrictions relate to that person's income. You are giving a gift to help them in retirement. Just an idea.

THINKING IT OVER

A final word about fairness and equally gifting. Some believe if they gift to one family member, they must give equally to others. Some only respond to a family member's "ask" for specific help. That does not obligate you to give the same amount to others. As we have said earlier, consider their financial track record. Are we spoiling, enabling, or giving to get something in return?

Make a list of gifts you would like to give, to whom, and where. Ask these questions: Will these hurt or help? Are they the best type of gift at the best time for the recipient?

God treats us equally, but uniquely. He creates appropriate expectations and gives grace. Helping others financially is worthy of our careful consideration and prayer. Remember, it is all God's, on loan to us, to manage wisely.

MARRIAGE AND MONEY

A cord of three strands is not quickly broken.

ECCLESIASTES 4:12

Whoever gives heed to instruction prospers,
and blessed is the one who trusts in the LORD.

PROVERBS 16:20

MARRIAGE AND MONEY—fireworks or fun?

Finances are cited as one of the greatest sources of disagreements, arguments, even a cause for divorce. The first is lack of communication, the second, money disagreements.[1] But money itself is not the problem. Money problems are a symptom of a heart issue. It could be greed, coveting, lack of faith, scarcity mentality, fear, desire for power, or laziness. Many heart issues are manifested in problems with money.

VALERIE SAYS . . .

When my husband and I married, our pastor quoted this verse: "A cord of three strands is not quickly broken" (Ecc. 4:12). Marriage, one man and one woman, agreeing to commit to

> *each other for a lifetime are two strands. That third strand is God. Before marriage, learn whether God's guidelines for money matter to that person. If not, do not marry. Closely examine the financial behavior of that person.*

Each person will bring their pattern of living into your marriage. Do they have credit card debt? Spend impulsively? Hoard to the extreme of harsh living? Are they generous, or not? Stating vows does not change the pattern. Determining and committing to that common bond of honoring God's guidelines carries you through tough challenges. And life has lots of those.

That common bond, the third strand of God, is your guideline. We go to God together when we make big and small decisions on living space, vehicles, furniture, kids' education, everything. We talk, pay attention to where income is coming from and where it is going. Proverbs 16:20 says, "Whoever gives heed to instruction prospers, and blessed is the one who trusts in the LORD." We cannot stress this enough. Be attentive, pay attention to **all** income, and **all** money going out, together.

PAY ATTENTION!

These discussions are vital before marriage. Each person needs to come clean about credit card debt, student loans, even credit scores. These realities will affect your lifestyle as a couple. Bringing debt into marriage may seem insignificant until other challenges come. And as we have said, life has lots of those.

A case can be made for prenuptial agreements. This is not a matter of love or selfishness. It is acknowledging the reality of different backgrounds, possible previous marriages with children, and respect. I know of widows who have married widowers and desire that their children inherit wealth from her marriage to their father. The same is true for women who are divorced and remarry, or are marrying a man who has children. A prenuptial agreement provides for this. Rather than being disruptive to the marriage, that agreement can provide protection and wise stewardship given life's unknowns.

Prenuptial agreements can provide a foundation of comfort not just for the couple, but for their children.

> **MIRIAM SAYS . . .**
>
> *Being real here, when I speak to gatherings of widows, I often have them repeat after me, "After the hearse, don't be a purse or a nurse." Yes, people laugh. But there is much wisdom for both widows and widowers remarrying.*

While a case can be made for separate bank accounts for a young couple, there still must be transparency. In one such instance the wife could not understand why her husband's account was often negative. Finally she learned he was a gambler. Being married, she was responsible for his debt. Transparency is a must.

Single young women, be smart. If you are considering marrying a person, let your Board of Directors vet him. Your board member who shares financial wisdom with you is a good resource. Marriage is not an experiment. It's a covenant commitment. We say, "In God we trust. All others bring documentation." This may sound harsh. Remember we're committed to being wise.

If you are single and contemplating marriage, better to determine your expectations in a future commitment in order to first honor God, and then be assured that He will guide you.

If you are engaged, young or any age, we recommend going together to a class on finances. You'll learn much and either embark on smoother financial sailing in marriage, or not continue in that relationship.

Widows have contacted us, having discovered after their husband's death, that unknown to her, he owed thousands in credit card debt, or even gambling debt. One woman, who had never opened credit card bills, discovered she was now responsible for $100,000.00 in credit card debt from several sources.

Another widow, through marriage, lived modestly with both working. She was devastated when her husband committed suicide. Shortly after the funeral, she discovered he had accumulated large gambling debts. A collector came knocking. She was now responsible for those debts. These examples, while real, are hopefully rare. We share this to underline what we have been saying.

Attentive, together. Before marriage and throughout marriage. Prioritize, plan times, and keep them. Regularly!

A spouse or potential spouse who is secretive about money is a giant red flag. We have seen this play out time and time again when we are contacted by women who are wondering what happened, and how did they get to this place. Few people want to keep good news a secret for long. Let's think about it.

When it is time to talk about money, pick a time for discussions when things are smooth, not when you are tired or hungry. You will differ because you are two separate human beings. It is okay to disagree. If you agree on everything, one of you is unnecessary!

But another huge red flag—there is never a good time to talk about money. Another word for this is avoidance. Where money is coming from, where it has gone, where it is going and should go, need to be discussed often.

VALERIE SAYS . . .

In our house, we talk about money at least weekly.

Backgrounds shape us all differently. Whether talking about sizing down in space, revamping your budget because of changes, or how much to give, communicate, communicate, communicate. Hopefully, you have started these talks before marriage. If not, it is never too early to start. It is never wise to delay starting these discussions.

Compromise, pause, pray, and affirm what you can agree on. That unity, and assurance of the "why," will help you through so many upheavals.

> **VALERIE SAYS . . .**
> *In our marriage, when we do not agree on a purchase or money commitment, we do not proceed on it until both of us are "on board."*

If we are one, which Scripture says we are, then we should be united on major decisions. "For this reason a man will leave his father and mother and be **united** to his wife, and the two will become one flesh" (Eph. 5:31).

Or if you use the "equally yoked" analogy, it does not work well to be pulling in opposite directions or one being dragged along (2 Cor. 6:14). This is not sustainable. We would add this caveat to not moving forward without both agreeing. It is not okay for one spouse to keep the other from ever moving forward. That is not agreement and reasonable compromise; that is holding the other hostage. Just remember, this is your spouse. If God is on the throne of each of your hearts, and not yourself, this becomes easier. "My way or the highway" is not marriage.

THREE BIG THINGS

We suggest these three things that are vital in your marriage to master your finances:

1. Agree on a basic plan. Given what is coming in, what can go out? What matters to each of you? And why? We cannot stress enough a shared value of NOT accumulating debt and having an emergency fund. That alone will lessen later financial stresses and arguments. It is okay to have separate discretionary areas for nonessentials, not secret, just determined by one person.

Here is a practical example. I have a beauty section of the budget. Heaven knows, the older I get, it is essential. Mark is not interested in the least as to how much of that is for hair items, manicures, or face lotion. It is not that he cannot know, it is that the budget is set, and he does not care to know how the fine detail is worked out.

Another example, Mark likes to golf. I, to date, am not a fan. So, there is an area in the budget for golf. I do not care in the least how much of that is for golf balls, course fees, caddies (although we are usually not that fancy), or driving range practice. I know the overall budget amount and do not care how the details of that work out, as long as the caddie is not a supermodel.

2. Spend time together in regular and consistent budget work. That newlywed one-bedroom apartment is likely NOT your long-term home. How much home matters? Can we accumulate our emergency fund and have two new cars? We suggest attending a class, even online, like Financial Peace or Crown Financial. Meeting with a budget counselor might take the edge off touchy conversations and give an impartial perspective.

3. Be willing to change your habits. Really important. Marriage means compromise. Marriages simply do not thrive without it. Small stuff, home temperature, open windows, eating leftovers or throwing them out. Bigger stuff, he really wants that car. She is frugal and wants more savings for kids' college. Each person's opinion matters. It is better to kick around ideas, not demands. We like money conversations that include things like "a dream I have is to one day do . . . " or "this, to me, is more valuable than . . . "

It is of great importance to get to know what drives your spouse's worldview about making, saving, and spending money. If one of you says, "I want this," a great follow-up question (in a genuinely interested tone) is "What about that item do you like?" "Why is this important to you?"

> Money fast fact: Money is finite. When we choose to put money toward one thing, we are choosing not to put it toward another.

A fact about money is this—no matter who we are, we have a finite amount. When we choose to put money toward one thing, we are choosing not to put it toward another. One helpful exercise may be to make a money spending "wish list," which can include savings as a way to "spend," and then rank each item. Your spouse can do that too. Then share and do not criticize.

> Seek first to understand, then to be understood.

Both spouses are of equal value. Marriage should be fair and mutually beneficial. One person should not control everything, and one person should not always be giving in. We sincerely believe that God created each person to bring about

His purposes in the world. Marriage should be so empowering that it propels both in the marriage to greater ability to serve God and encourage human flourishing. Arguing over stuff and money does none of that.

Here is a word about second marriages. Statistics show they are more likely to fail than first marriages.[2] Shared unity about money is just as important now as for that first marriage. Sadly, we know women who swallowed the "we'll resolve that later" and regretted it. Prenuptial agreements might be wise, necessary, and promote peace in your second marriage. Wealth and debt might be different. These agreements are especially important in second marriages with blended families, and even adult children.

We cannot stress enough that transparency in marriage is a requirement. Spouses have told us they saw warning signals but did not want to face them. Death or divorce does not negate debts and responsibility of that person. "He's better at finances" or "I have tried to involve him, but he's not interested" are not excuses. As we have stated before, in 80% of marriages, the husband will die before the wife. So, 80% of the time, she WILL do the finances, ready, interested, competent, or not. Husbands, share the information. Ladies, he married an adult, so get in there and learn. And where appropriate, switch up the involvement.

Guys can be uninterested in finance and women can be over-controlling. We are simply calling it like we see it. Statistics on financial health of women versus men after divorce or death of a spouse reveal that women are not positioned as well as men financially.[3] We are not being sexist; we are existing in reality.

THINKING IT OVER

Talk, be alert, be transparent. Courage, my friend. Transparency and addressing the problem, including God in the process can lessen crisis ahead.

If you are married, how do your "money talks" go? Do you know your spouse's learning style—a spreadsheet or pie chart? If you are not married, do you have a trusted confidant about money? How do those talks go?

We have acknowledged that it is all God's—our combined incomes, all we have. God sees your attempts as a couple to steward what is His together. Gain courage by knowing that you matter to Him, your marriage matters to Him. He stands ready to help you.

13

EMOTIONS: BUDGET BUSTERS

Commit to the Lord whatever you do,
and he will establish your plans.

PROVERBS 16:3

The fear of the Lord leads to life;
then one rests content, untouched by trouble.

PROVERBS 19:23

If any of you is lacks wisdom, you should ask God, who gives
generously to all without finding fault, and it will be given you.

JAMES 1:5

FINANCIAL SUCCESS, becoming a wise woman managing money, is all about the mind and numbers. Right? Disciplined thinking and determining our spending plan are vital for sure. But there is more. We have said that debt is a greedy beast. Our emotions can increase that greedy beast's appetite. Emotions impact our decisions and even empower or destroy our ability to do what our mind says is wise.

MIRIAM SAYS . . .

In my counseling years and personal life, I can say emotions are a powerful force. You probably know that too. Money can ring that bell of anger, fear, jealousy, happiness, and greed. In turn, emotions like anger, disappointment, loneliness, and others can bust our budget. We try to soothe that emotion with a purchase, outside the bumper pads of our budget.

We are hoping that you've created a spending plan based on the rock-solid foundation of God's word. In chapter 2, we talked about changes that shake our world. A reality of life is that storms will happen. Most are unwelcome, some the result of our own choices. Emotions heighten the storm, intensify the damage, and can bust our budget.

Let's look at a few examples to give us a heads-up so we recognize potential budget busters.

- **Disappointment:** Impulse, I owe it to myself—splurge. I am hurting—retail therapy to the rescue. The mall, shopping online . . . fill the void with stuff.

- **Anger in marriage:** He did that! Not right! I am off with our credit card to take care of me.

- **Comparison and feeling inadequate:** If I just had a nicer car, I would be treated with more respect like he/she is . . .

Worry is another budget busting emotion. Consider that the average worker spends 150 hours a year worrying about money. That loss of productivity results in a $250 billion loss.

Eighty-four percent of companies are now offering debt management tools and other resources.[1] Companies realize that worry costs money. That worry drains us emotionally, even physically. A 2016 study found that 85% of adults in the United States feel financial anxiety—up 33% over the previous 3 years. Sixty-nine percent have less than $1,000 in a savings account.[2]

Buying does not fix disappointment; revenge buying does not satisfy anger. Buying to keep up with another does not work, and worry does not earn any money. Done! Fixed!

One survey, produced by Capital One, found that 77% of Americans are anxious about their financial situation, 58% feel their finances control their lives rather than the other way around, and 52% have difficulty controlling money-related worries.[3] And this study was before the COVID-19 pandemic storm that followed.

Does this impact relationships? Certainly! Irritability, feeling overwhelmed, distracted and unable to concentrate—family, friends, all social interactions are affected. As we stated earlier, some studies show financial issues are the second leading cause for divorce.[4]

When we base our spending plan on God's principles, following it gives us a sense of peace. We have more hours to spend being productive, not worrying.

Be especially careful in transition times, especially hard ones. Divorce, loss of an important relationship, death of a child or widowhood are times of vulnerability, finances included.

You feel like you are in a financial shark tank. Money is snapped up by the unexpected. You may feel numb, like you do not care. Still, that shark grabbing money will cost you more pain. Heads up. Do not feed the sharks.

Even in chaos, pay attention. Check your credit card statements for unexpected charges and pay on time. Monitor your bank balance. If you have automatic deductions and your income has changed, you need to make immediate changes or face the high costs of bank overdrafts. They may be as high as $35.00. You will begin to feel a bit of comfort and stability in the mundane tasks of paying attention.

Unwanted and unexpected change can trigger fear. People who have suffered a loss, divorce, or death of someone important especially, might become hoarders to fill that loss with stuff. Whether retail or garage sale, stuff does not satisfy. It even blinds us to the **real** source of contentment, Jesus Himself who knows, cares, and comforts.

KNOW IT AND OWN IT

Recognizing that emotions are impacting our financial reality is a vital first step. Denial and avoidance are never productive solutions. If you are recognizing this reality in your own circumstance, reach out for help.

Here are three suggested resources. Go to your Board of Directors (chapter 2) and get counsel from those trusted people who can give insights into your finances and your anxiety. The decision rests with YOU as to what to heed and what to ignore. A trusted person who knows you well, has your best interests at heart, and who has common sense, will likely give you great and straight insights.

Another possible resource is professional help from a financial advisor. We walk with you in making that selection in chapter 18. You may or may not need this person. That chapter will help you decide. If you conclude that you need this professional, that chapter will help you in choosing the right person for you.

A third possibility is getting professional help for emotional turmoil.

MIRIAM SAYS . . .

I understand its importance and value. It was my profession. They may be licensed therapists or counselors, psychologists, and psychiatrists, and others as well.

Here is what these professionals can and cannot do:

- They can help you identify sources of your problems, clarify and see other choices. They can validate straight thinking, and some (psychiatrists) can prescribe medication when appropriate.

- They cannot change your circumstances, or fix your past. They cannot create your future, or change you.

Emotions can be positive in that time of change. Do you have an item that is tied to a positive memory or has sentimental value? Keeping that visible during emotional upheavals can help you be wise. I have a fossilized rock from a stream on our farm. Maybe once it was a knot on a tree. Just seeing it reminds me of carefree days wandering through a stream. I look at my rock and think peace, frugality, stability, splashing freedom. All will be okay. Scripture is full of reminders. God is our real rock.

CHANGE IT

It is important to address one more challenge regarding emotions and finances. Emotions are stubborn things, even habitual, even if they bring negative outcomes. Helpful or harmful, habits are tough to break.

Helpful—we routinely start a vehicle, brush our teeth, no thought.

Harsh—we spend on something we don't need or simply waste money. We do the same thing. A good plan of action is like Ready, Aim, Fire. A bad habit is, fire first and then try to recover from the consequence. Spending has a parallel. Good habit: Plan, Compare, Buy. Bad habit: Buy, then borrow and regret the consequences.

What triggers that purchase? Scrolling online, entering that favorite store. Change the habit. Shopping is not a good form of entertainment. It brings discontent, debt, then regret and waste. Not our top choices in entertainment. Resist that trigger and replace it with what calms your soul. For us, it is a brisk walk, a time of solitude. Yours might be exercise or recreational reading, creating art, or hobby time.

Compose your own Scripture list of God's wisdom that applies personally to you and your emotional challenge. The enemies of budget busters are: wisdom from God, knowing your worth comes from God and not what you have or make, and planning in advance. You cannot make a rash and impulsive purchase that you have been planning for months. By definition, that is impossible. So, go ahead, make that Christmas list in July, make your wish list and wait a week, or month, to buy things on it, save for that tire before it is bald. Think it through. Hurried purchases when you are upset, worn out, hungry, or depressed are almost always regretted. Take your burdens to the Lord, not to the store!

Ask God for wisdom to guide your mind in changing that habit. James 1:5 tells us, "If any of you lacks wisdom, you should ask God, who gives generously to all without finding fault, and it will be given you." That is God's promise.

THINKING IT OVER

We suggest that you make a list of items you recently bought that you wish you could return or were an impulse spend. What was the rationale for buying that item at that moment? Was it really about needing the item?

Another important question to ponder is this: Do I see a pattern here? Identifying the thought or rationale that leads to that budget buster is an important discovery. You aren't only NOT feeding the sharks, you are now able to stay out of, far away from, the shark tank.

14

FINANCIAL FRAUD

So if you have not been trustworthy in handling worldly wealth,
who will trust you with true riches?

BIG INCOME? Financial windfall? Life insurance? Inherited money? Someone has a plan for your money! For their profit, not yours.

Financial fraud is common. It is common for someone who just earned a huge salary, inherited money, or received a windfall, to be targeted by financial fraudsters. Statistics tell us that many lottery winners are poor within years. Athletes who earned millions are later without resources. If you are in transition, you are a target. Widowed and recently a recipient of money? Someone has a plan for your money, for their profit, not yours. Fraud is big business, so how do we spot it?

Almost always the appeal is emotional. The gist of their argument is "you deserve this. After what you have gone through, we will watch over this for you." Sadly, that is seldom the truth. For your protection—do NOT act hastily. Tell them you will not be making a decision until you have fact checked their proposal and discussed it with trusted advisors, which may include a lawyer and financial planner. Vet all professionals. You have no obligation to return a phone call or even answer their call. We advise that you never meet alone with someone who wants to talk about your money. We suggest you take someone along who you trust if you have such a person in your life. Someone who has your best interest at heart. Fraudsters often use tactics where they get you isolated, in a hurry, and emotionally involved. And they are good at it. Really good. They make their whole living by doing this, so—run!

Let's review a basic, biblical foundational truth. The job of managing your money, or property, or portfolio is yours to steward. It is all God's resources and yours, but just on loan. You need to understand and *can* understand the product or investment you make. If it is more complex, do not invest until you can research and understand it yourself. The financial fraudster will run when they see your due diligence and that you are including the checks and balances of comparison shopping and including wise counsel.

Sadly, there are those in the Christian community with greedy intent, or just foolish ideas. Christians can be trusting when they should not be. And vulnerable, especially if they are isolated. Women who are alone are especially vulnerable. One "Christian" man we knew set up a "bank" promising 14% on investments. Deacons, pastors, thousands invested. The bank collapsed. Lifetime savings disappeared. Knowing someone does not mean trusting them. There is a whole type of fraud called "affinity fraud." That is fraud by someone you are acquainted with, or have a common bond with such as someone from your church, alma mater, etc. Why are we so focused on protecting you from scams that take what God has entrusted to you? Because we hear of so many who have been taken advantage of, have been stolen from, lost everything—even enter poverty, or bankruptcy, due to being fooled into giving another person access to their resources.

One woman gave her bank passwords over the phone to a man who regularly called her to chat in her loneliness. Another wired her life savings to a new "friend" who had a "life-threatening illness" and needed funds for treatment. Another was pushed to put her children's college money in a poorly rated mutual fund. One widow bought partial ownership in a new restaurant with all of her life insurance. It failed. These real stories break our hearts. Not to mention those women could have used those resources to self-sustain, and give. They could have moved from a five-talent steward to a ten-talent steward, but now they are no-talent stewards. In many of these cases, a simple check-in with wise counsel would have prevented disaster.

What protections do you have? While our government has some regulations, do not assume your "investment opportunity" is protected. Investing in fluff companies, even public companies riddled with dishonesty, is a threat. Enron is an example that looked good until they folded; it was a publicly traded company. We stress: investigate! Look at the fundamentals and technicalities of an investment.

Talk to respected financial professionals, folks who are following biblical principles with money, people with "common sense," which is often uncommon. Then wait. Hit the pause button. The person pushing an investment will want you to hurry and make a decision. But their "urgency" is not your "emergency."

You can add a name on to your portfolio, that of a trusted contact person through whom all asks and transfers must be approved. Forms are available with letters of instruction with limited specific access to your accounts and information only through that person.

Christ followers protect the vulnerable among us: elderly, widowed, orphans, disabled. People with dementia are especially vulnerable due to social isolation and mental impairment. Who notices? Scammers, strangers, nursing home staff, even, sadly, ill-intentioned family members. Taking advantage of the vulnerable is not following Christ, and in many cases, it is criminal. Many times scammers get away with evil for a long time because victims are embarrassed by their mistake. But do not let someone else suffer too. Shout it from the rooftops! Find your voice, and eat a little humble pie about the embarrassment. You are not the bad guy here, the fraudster is! It is okay. You will be a hero for someone else in the end. And if someone confides in you that they were taken advantage of, do not shame them. Encourage them to report it. God can use that experience in anyone's life for good in the end. When we go through something tough, we often emerge with both a hardened strength, and compassion for those who go through something similar.

We have another protection: trusting God to meet our needs, comfort us in our loneliness. He has the power to protect us from our own human stuff like greed. Financial fraudsters cannot be successful when we are content with what we have, including our circumstances.

And here are more resources to learn about fraud and to report it:

- Federal Trade Commission website and links to learn about/report fraud.

- Your state's Attorney General's office.

- You can even contact police at their non-emergency number to ask about fraud or to report it in your area.

Imagine the good we can do with money entrusted to us if we steward it wisely. That $100,000 wired to the scam artist, the $250,000 invested in the failed restaurant. The list goes on. Generosity to a God-honoring ministry or church, college tuition for a relative, helping a friend through a rough patch in life? God has entrusted us with all that we have. Our goal is to become wise women managing money.

THINKING IT OVER

This is so important that we are providing a quick re-cap. Have you witnessed any of these marks of financial fraud? If so, which ones?

- ▶ Emotional appeal. You need this, you deserve this.

- ▶ Pressure to quickly sign or agree.

- ▶ Affinity fraud. I am in the same church, golf group, even a relative!

- ▶ Return on investment is too good to be true!

- ▶ Predators of "vintage" people and those with dementia.

Remember these protections:

- ▶ Hit the pause button.

- ▶ Investigate, investigate, investigate.

- ▶ Research and vet ALL individuals.

- ▶ Common sense: take time to noodle and ponder.

- ▶ Check government websites such as the Federal Trade Commission or State's Attorney General for current scams.

- ▶ Add a trusted name to your portfolio and accounts.

God has entrusted us with all that we have. Our goal, to become wise women managing money.

DANGER! FILLING OUR VOID WITH "STUFF" OR PEOPLE

For where your treasure is, there your heart will be also.

MATTHEW 6:21

WE HAVE TALKED about potential budget busters—our emotions and financial fraud. Sneaky budget busters for sure. Here is another: our stuff.

We have been acquiring wisdom for managing our money. We have come a long way. We have a spending plan; we are working our plan and staying true to our "why." How can "stuff" be a budget buster? Let's get perspective.

Becoming wise women managing money, we know our best guidebook is the Bible. With more than two thousand references to money, it is important. The only other more referenced topic is love. We think first of that bank account, or property, or portfolio. But Scripture refers to much more. It is about our stuff—what is in our closet, cabinets, tool sheds, storage units and more. We might call it the "Bigger Barn Syndrome."

> Bigger Barn Syndrome: Having too much grain
> (or other stuff) to keep for yourself means you have to
> build a bigger barn. (Luke 12:16–21)

We may not see stuff as valuable, or even important. But let's look at the bigger picture. Why did we get it, why do we keep it, and how much of our time and energy does stuff consume?

Let's talk numbers. Forty-eight percent of Americans say their homes are cluttered with things they no longer use. Nearly half think they have unused items worth more than $1,000.00.[1] Almost 10% of American households rent a storage unit, which costs over $1,000 annually.[2]

Does that stuff have a near-future use for us? If so, that is okay. But let's look a bit deeper. *Hoarders* was a popular television show. Scanning a room so crammed with stuff it was unusable, the team attempted to clear out the clutter. The owner, who was suffering from too much stuff, provided the greatest resistance. With only narrow pathways through rooms, family and friends no longer coming over, they were paying a price— but clung to their stuff. Why? That stuff was comfort, filling a void in that person's life.

We may not be that extreme, but our temptation is to fill voids in our lives with stuff. Hoarding is a common one. By definition, it is spending and keeping stuff for comfort, or other emotional need, not the item's usefulness.

We accumulate at great expense to our wallet and less comfort in our living space. Hoarding is self-centered and excessive. It impairs mobility and interferes with basic activity. Let's shine biblical truth on that. It is God's money and stuff, not ours. Having unused stuff is being like the steward in Matthew 25 who was given one talent and hid it, like putting money in a shoebox or burying it underground.

Remember Jesus' words in Luke 12:15, "Then he said to them, 'Watch out! Be on your guard against all kinds of greed; life does not consist in an abundance of possessions.'"

Here is another temptation. Handing out: Giving stuff as a gift, giving it out, to get something back.

We hand out to get something in return that we think will make us feel good. A better word might be "bribe." Handing out is giving something to another person that costs you something and is of value to you, in the hope that they will stay in your life, or invest in your life, do what you want them to do, helping to fill your personal void.

We have a better option. Bless another person with that stuff freely—no strings attached. Donate it. Someone else will not have to purchase new. Possibilities are endless: slightly used, or no-longer-fits clothing, second set of kitchenware, children's toys, household decor stuff, even bedding. Empty that storage unit and give to a worthy cause. Declutter the space so you do not have to dust, oil, or repair that unused item. You may even be able to downsize your space once you get rid of your clutter. Then you will not have to mortgage it, heat or air-condition it, insure it . . .

Garage sales are still an option, but selling online has become popular. Craigslist, eBay, and Facebook expand selling to more buyers. Furniture, collectibles, it is all there. If you do not need the money the sale brings, donate those dollars to a worthy charity.

One thousand dollars buys four new treadle sewing machines for widows we train in Africa. To them, it is not stuff. It is a new lease on financial independence.

Get a friend's perspective. Invite them into your living space. What do they see? Ask them this question: "Looking around my living room, or closet, what do you think I value?" "Stuff" is not evil. God gives us richly all things to enjoy. For sure, we need food and clothing, but too much distracts us, and consumes us.

As our MDiv (Master of Divinity) friend says, "First time by flood, then by fire." It will all eventually burn. That is pretty harsh, but not incorrect. "Stuff" is temporary. People are eternal. Treasure each other, the people God has created in His image, and God Himself first. He is our real treasure.

CAN A PERSON FILL A VOID?

May we offer one more caution when that void in our lives calls out to be filled? Just as stuff does not fill a void, neither does a person. Do not expect any person to be the answer. Becoming divorced or widowed leaves a hole in our hearts, our calendars, our lives, and often our wallets.

MIRIAM SAYS . . .

I understand. My husband going to heaven after forty-two years of marriage left a huge void. Within two months, my retirement date meant my job surrounded by people ended. I understand lonely. But heal first, be that whole person, before looking around.

Filling that void with another person is to invite dashed expectations. Just as acquiring stuff to fill a void does not work, neither is filling it with another person. This will likely be a costly dashed expectation.

Jennifer was a newly divorced mom of two. The divorce meant she was on her own financially, and seldom received needed child support. Her job was adequate, but things were always tight. Enter Mr. Wonderful, who seemed to love her company and built her self-esteem at a vulnerable time.

She did not notice that he had often "forgotten" his credit card after a meal out. Months into the relationship, he hit a financial bump (supposedly) and asked her for a loan! She had some meager savings and complied. Poof! The person and her small purse of savings disappeared. Bad idea.

Sadly, second marriages for divorcees and widows can be bumpy as well. One widow told us she would have not married that second time, which ended in divorce, had she fully healed and become whole on her own first, before entering a new relationship. Yes, the divorce was financially costly as well as painful.

Okay, girls, this sounds funny, but it is serious. Like we said before, if you are widowed, after the hearse, don't become a purse or a nurse. Don't let in new "friends" that are really budget busters.

A few golden friends are better than lots of people. And God knows every corner and crevice of your empty heart. He can fill it.

Those of you who are minimalists need not read further. But if you have determined "stuff" is a distraction, requiring too much time and money to keep up, here are suggestions.

Assess the value of things you no longer need. It is common to believe memorabilia, even antiques, are worth more than real market value. Internet research helps in determining what sells and for how much. An item is only worth what someone is willing to pay for it. Classic law of supply and demand.

One acquaintance clung to his stuff thinking, hoping, to get more than anyone would offer. Result: his home appeared like that of a hoarder. Some rooms had only a path through them.

MIRIAM SAYS . . .
We think that is extreme. But I, being the vintage writer here, found myself shuffling through many jackets (mostly unused) to find my favorite.

THINKING IT OVER

Dedicate a regular, reasonable amount of time to move stuff elsewhere. Even three hours a week is a good beginning. Out the door to a worthwhile place like consignment store, donation site, or garbage. Whether donated or sold, repurposing stuff is gratifying.

An added benefit to this exercise is that our wish list changes, even our spending plan. Categories shrink due to our newfound freedom. Why do we want it, why would we keep it, and how much of our time and energy will it consume? We find ourselves buying more intentionally which usually means less. And we can now get rid of those storage shelves as well.

Another action step is to intentionally let God fill that void.

"For where your treasure is, there your heart will be also" (Matt. 6:21).

CRISIS EQUALS OPPORTUNITY

Your path led through the sea, your way through the mighty waters,
though your footprints were not seen.

PSALM 77:19

WE WANT TO BECOME WISE women managing money. But our realities get tough at times. That means crisis happens, and it is usually unwelcome. We have learned over time that crisis can become our opportunity to do things we did not do before, could not do before.

Recognizing that research shows that women lack financial confidence, combine that with a change, even crisis, what we typically see is trouble ahead. Yet, we are saying crisis is an opportunity. We are not saying it is fun, easy, glamorous, or quickly embraceable. It is opportunity usually well-disguised.

CRISIS REVEALS WHO WE TRUST

One foundational, biblical truth is this: Each of us is uniquely created in God's image.

As His image bearers, we have capacities yet unexplored, resilience, skills yet to be developed, and His resources to depend on and use as we trust Him. It has been said, "He creates the back for the burden." Scripture is full of examples of people who faced upheavals that might have destroyed them. Yet, they moved forward in unexpected and God-blessed ways—David the shepherd (later king), Bathsheba, Abigail, the prophetess Anna, and prophetess Deborah. We will list these at the end of this chapter.

Looking squarely at the crisis, our culture encourages us to look only within ourselves for strength and solutions. Our culture says we can have it all and make it all happen. All we need is within us.

Simply stated, that belief sets us up for failure. Our greatest source for all we need is our Lord. Crisis reveals our trust, our faith, even when we are moving forward in spite of doubts many times. We call it stepping out on shaky legs. "So take a new grip with your tired hands, stand firm on your shaky legs" (Heb. 12:12 TLB).

We state this truth (the fact of our weakness) first and embrace the truth that we CAN explore, step in, and embrace this new opportunity. We will expand on this as we go.

We understand that you may doubt this. When we lack financial confidence, we hesitate to explore, and step in, let alone embrace a new opportunity.

CRISIS PROVIDES AN OPPORTUNITY TO LEARN

Consider these women's experiences:

Diane, in divorce proceedings, discovered that her husband had incurred gambling debts. She had to share the responsibility to repay those as they were incurred during her marriage. After the anger dissipated, she put her shoulder to the plow. (An old farm term for getting down to business.)

After the divorce, she gained a new confidence in that decisions were hers. She gained peace based on predictability she did not have before. She is on sound financial footing today. Opportunity: financial confidence.

Young widow Nancy's husband had been a handyman fixing everything. After his death, she said, "I had lots of tools. I just didn't know how to use them."

"I had lots of tools. I just didn't know how to use them."

Now she rides her lawnmower, hangs pictures, and drills closet walls to hang shelves. How often do we learn when we need to! It is so true with managing money. If we have not been doing it, we did not learn and grow those skills. If you are going through a rough patch in life, a transition that requires change, your finances can be worrisome. You are required to step up.

Crisis can bring danger but can also bring opportunity.

MIRIAM SAYS . . .

God is creative in His plan for us. Becoming a widow and retired, I thought I would transition to teaching in a university. That door had already opened. But God had a different plan. I am training widows in developing countries in a self-sustaining

> *skill, managing my own portfolio, and loving it. My goal and plan? No, but better than anything I could imagine.*

Transition or crisis time, we can assure you of this refreshing discovery: We are more resilient than we think. How do we know? Scripture tells us we are uniquely formed. We established this earlier. When God created us, He knew each day of our lives. Today's upheaval is no surprise to Him.

CRISIS REVEALS OUR TRUE FRIENDS

Sharon, being single and believing her income would continually increase, found herself "overcommitted and underfunded." Something had to change. Family members denied her requests for money. Understandably, they did not want to enable her financial behavior.

As she could no longer afford the entertainment and vacations with friends, as well as other "over her budget" activities, she found her "friendship" circle shrinking. She eventually realized "fun stuff only" friends were not real friends. Opportunity: financial accountability, and meaningful friendships.

New friends will be discovered in new ways and in new places. We learn from others. We network and explore online. Review our Board of Directors recommendation in chapter 2. Connect with those who have gone through similar struggles. Our friendship network usually shrinks initially, but we can grow it in a meaningful way.

THREE KINDS OF FRIENDS

MIRIAM SAYS . . .

As my friendship network quaked and shrank, I went to Scripture to understand. I learned there were three different words in the original languages that are translated "friend" —each very different.

First, Philos (noun): one who loves (Prov. 17:9; 18:24). This friend has your back. Loves you no matter what.

Second, Hetairos (noun): a comrade/companion/partner (Prov. 18:24). This is a convenient friendship, similar interests that might not exist after your crisis.

Third, Peitho (verb): to persuade, influence (Prov. 14:20). This is a user friend. If relating to you no longer benefits them, they are gone. [1]

Those categories translate to getting advice related to money. Who advises us for our best interest? Who just has some common interests and shares their "wisdom"? And who is a user and wants to take advantage of us in our time of turmoil?

Take time to reconsider what you value. You cannot have the past back. What would you like your future to look like? Crisis time can be fresh-start time. Revisit the chart in chapter 9 called "Rating Your Life Values." You rated the sixteen key values that people often say they want to experience. Which values would rate highly today given this crisis in your life? It is not unusual for upheavals to change our focus, even change our life path.

What we value can get squeezed out in some seasons of life. What mom prioritizes taking care of her own health? Empty nest time can be opportunity time. Women have found themselves now the owner of companies, at the helm of a new adventure.

THINKING IT OVER

We can assure you, putting your dependence and trust in God, here is what you can expect:

> God will act,
> act in His time,
> suffer with us,
> and prevail.

In frugal financial times, we see His provision in unexpected ways. Delays are times of faith building, prayer muscle building, and discovering other people with compassion.

Be encouraged by these examples.

Anna, widowed young and childless, became a revered prophetess. She prayed and fasted daily in the temple rather than remarrying. She saw Jesus, the babe, her Messiah, and proclaimed Him to all. (Luke 2)

Bathsheba, a widow, married the man responsible for the murder of Uriah, her husband. That devastating crisis did not prevent her from fulfilling her new calling. She fulfilled the unexpected mission of parenting the next king: King Solomon. (2 Sam. 11–12)

Abigail was the wife of a wealthy but ill-natured man. Widowhood resulted in her remarrying, and later her husband David became king. Freed from her marriage to an abusive man, her next husband attained a more revered position. What transitions! (1 Sam. 25)

Deborah, as a judge and prophetess, admonished Barak to go to war. He refused unless she rode with him. From presiding under a tree, to horseback at the front of the battle lines, Deborah rose to the new challenge. Result, she sang a new song to acknowledge what God had led her to do. (Judges 4–5)

David, the shepherd boy killed animals with his slingshot. He later killed Goliath with the same skill. Then he became skilled with swords and more. (1 Sam. 17)

Reflect on how God has provided for you in unexpected ways.

Trust this truth. Psalm 77:19 says, "Your path led through the sea, your way through the mighty waters, though your footprints were not seen." The day will come, in heaven, perhaps not before, when you see through it all that God had your back.

INVE$TING

In this section we will do a deep dive into topics we have mentioned earlier. Let's review. We know what we have. We are working our plan to manage it well and we have faced the realities of budget-busters in our life.

Now it's fun time. Let's grow our financial literacy to a new level. In chapter 5, we did a brief overview of where to store (money) assets. We will dig deeper here into the decision-making process of where we want our assets to be, what tools we want to create for changing seasons of our life, and where we would like our assets to go after we die. Fact: 100% sure reality that we will leave this planet at some time.

If you are feeling a twinge of hesitation, that it might be challenging, not quite for you, this perspective might help— God entrusted to you what you have. He would not put what He owns and values into your hands except that He knows you are able to steward it well. You have God's vote of confidence. What more do you need?

KNOWLEDGE, GOALS, RISK TOLERANCE

Dishonest money dwindles away,
but whoever gathers money little by little makes it grow.

PROVERBS 13:11

IN THIS CHAPTER, we want to grow our knowledge to manage our investments for short, long, and beyond our life, time frames. We will not make recommendations on which section of the investment "grocery store" is right for you. However, the more you know of those sections, the better decisions you will make.

You have probably heard many of the terms and concepts we will discuss here. We hope you will have a greater grasp not just of the terms, but their benefits and functions. Just good foundational information for stewards today.

That God entrusts us with assets is a privilege. With that comes responsibility. If you are thinking of ducking the responsibility, which we call opportunity, think again.

You expect us to be direct, right? Here are some excuses that do not work . . .

I never did this before.

I am not interested.

Someone else will do it for me.

Don't bother me. (or: I don't understand, it's too complex)

Got no time for this.

Consider this. You are cruising down the interstate, let's say in a convertible, hair blowing in the wind, soaking up the sun.

You hear a siren. A car is gaining on you with red flashing lights. Surely, they will fly by you and be on their way.

Oops, it's me! They are pulling me over. "Ma'am, did you know you were going a hundred miles per hour?"

"Really?" Inner thought: *I wasn't paying attention.*

"Ma'am, did you know the speed limit on this interstate is 65 miles per hour?"

Me: "Oh, I didn't know that. I won't go that fast again. Surely you won't give me a ticket. I just didn't know. I'll watch for those signs next time."

"Ma'am, here's your ticket. Knowing the speed limit is the responsibility of anyone driving a car."

We have made the point. Scripture says we are a steward overseeing what God has entrusted to us. That means paying attention to our finances is a God assignment. Something to do intentionally, with purpose.

MIRIAM SAYS . . .

I consider this one of the most fun chapters in this book!

VALERIE SAYS . . .

Mom, in addition to being a word nerd, you're becoming a numbers nerd. Like me!

KNOWLEDGE

Let's quickly review timelines from chapter 5. Funds you need *soon* need to be relatively safe and available. Think bank account or money market. Money needed *later* depends on expected time needed. If you need it in three to five years, it may be wiser to expose it to greater investment risk for greater gains. Typically we look in the equities (stocks, mutual funds) or bonds section. As we stated in chapter 5, S&P's 10–11% average historical growth is an example.[1]

Given this three- or five-year time frame, let's learn differences in sizes of companies. Conveniently, they are labeled as large-cap, mid-cap, and small-cap stocks. Let's dig in.

Large-cap stocks have a market capitalization of $10 billion or more. (That means the total worth of that company—as determined by the stock market.) They tend to be less volatile. They often pay dividends. They are likely to be havens during rough markets due to their quality and stability. Examples are Johnson & Johnson, Coca-Cola, and Google.

Small-cap stocks have a market capitalization of between $300 million and $2 billion. They are generally seen as riskier than large-cap stocks, have greater growth potential, and tend to offer better returns over the long term. They tend to be newer, start-ups, like toddlers compared to large-cap adults. Seldom do they offer dividends, as they need earned funds to grow the company.

Mid-cap stocks are the in-betweeners. They typically have less volatility than small-caps, less growth potential as well. They have more growth potential than the lumbering large-caps and some volatility. We might call them teenagers.

Which has greater growth potential? More potential for bumps and bruises along the way?

Blue chip stocks are often large-cap stocks. They are huge companies with excellent reputations. Examples are IBM, Amazon, Apple, 3M, and AbbVie. They typically have dividends and are considered safe. How are they different from large-cap stocks? They may not be. Blue-chip stocks are in major market indexes. Market indexes are a grouping of companies that represent a type of stock, or a section of the whole stock market. Some commonly referenced indexes are the Dow Jones, the S&P 500, and the NASDAQ. In very general terms, these represent large-cap stocks, the overall market, and tech stocks respectively. These indexes are frequently used as a "benchmark" or way to compare an individual stock in that category.

> Dividends are regular payments made to investors from a company's revenue. Mature companies can offer them because they no longer need to invest as much revenue back into their growth.[2]

Funds needed twenty to forty years later can likely weather greater ups and downs in order to capture greater gains. Why? Because there is more time to wait in their up/down cycle. You do not have to sell that stock soon. Look again at our grocery analogy in chapter 5. As you become better acquainted with these options, you will hear discussions with greater insight and read articles absorbing even more. That longer time frame typically means you can have a mixture of large, medium, and small-cap stocks.

RISK TOLERANCE

We are all different. No surprise here. Fact: Our risk tolerance is different. We have a friend who was widowed when her children were small. She worked consistently and had a small portfolio for retirement. An advisor gave oversight. Then the gyrations of 2007 hit the markets and real estate. She panicked and told the advisor to get her out of everything. He did so. She simply did not have the "stomach" to weather ups and downs. With her money all in money markets, she missed the markets' total rebound, going even higher over the next few years.

We are not saying her decision was right or wrong. If sleepless nights and wringing hands prevail, no other person should insist that she endure that. Nor would she want that for herself.

The result of her decision was that her portfolio did not grow. She would have had more in the future for living and giving. But she had no risk tolerance and was content with what she had.

As our financial literacy grows, we are able to make better decisions. Had she known more of what was in her portfolio, its risk factors, and market fluctuations, she might have made a different decision rather than panic in the moment. We do not know. Hindsight is always 20/20.

One important factor in determining risk tolerance for investments is what other sources do you have and/or will you have? If your investment plan is mainly for retirement income, will you have other income streams as well?

Two common retirement income sources are pensions and Social Security. Pensions are typically from federal government positions and some private companies. Social Security is not a pension, but is similar.

Pensions are becoming less common. Social Security benefits are expected to shrink. Should you have either of these, consider whether they are adequate for retirement. We frequently say KNOW IT. There are online predictors that may be helpful. Knowing at least a prediction of what will be available to you is a start.

Given that these sources may be small or nonexistent, a growing source of savings for retirement are IRA or 401(k) plans. Many companies offer employees the option of income going directly into the fund of withholding BEFORE TAXES. We like this. These funds go into the plan, not to be touched until retirement. Many companies match this. Free money. We like this a lot.

We can think of no reason not to participate in these if available to you.

A 401(k) plan is a tax-advantaged, defined-contribution retirement account offered by many employers to their employees. Workers contribute through automatic payroll deductions.[3]

You typically cannot pick individual stocks in a 401(k). It is more likely that they offer you a list of funds to choose from. Most include large-cap stock funds. Some are ETFs—exchange-traded funds—meaning a computer algorithm decides when to buy and sell stock in them. Some are actively managed, meaning a human is doing the buying and selling. Do some research before making those choices. (More about ETFs below.) Compare return rates, costs within the fund, and choose what is a match for you.

Peg and Sara are coworkers and friends. Peg is single. Sara is divorced. Both were offered a 401(k) in their workplace. What to choose, what to choose? Peg had a friend in finance. She asked him to review their choices. He pointed out the differences in their choices. He then recommended that they choose the greater growth option. They were both at least ten years from retirement time and could last through ups and downs in order to capture greater growth.

They are thrilled with the growth of their funds! They are watching and learning, growing financial literacy, as well as growing income for retirement.

Given that we change jobs more frequently than in the past, you can usually take that 401(k) with you, rolling it into an IRA or another 401(k) offered at your new job.

Participating in a 401(k) plan is a good beginning. One great benefit is that it is a learning tool. You get information on its growth, which draws your mind further into learning mode. It is yours so you pay attention. In chapter 22, we will dig deeper in the role these might play in your financial plans.

Consider your 401(k) a tasty item in your investing "grocery cart."

Portfolio: a range of investments held by a person or organization.

Let's talk about establishing a portfolio.

Becoming a widow, I was solely responsible for what God had entrusted to me. I chose to select a financial advisor to partner with me for this. We will spend the next chapter on how to make that selection. Briefly, for our purposes here, I chose one who was a part of an investment firm (company). They were a broker-dealer, meaning they bought and sold securities for clients (broker), and executed trades for their own benefit (dealer). That meant my portfolio was within that firm. Could I have gone lone ranger and set up my own? Sure. Examples are E*TRADE or TD Ameritrade. This is a broker offering a trading platform, and they do have tools for beginners. You are on your own to pick, buy, and sell. I simply was not prepared or informed enough to do that at that time.

Whether going with an established brokerage firm, through a bank, or on your own, begin at your comfort level. Yes, that choice of having someone else manage your investments has costs greater than doing it yourself. Make sure you know those costs when choosing a financial advisor.

We were with a brokerage firm with set fees and offering advice on equities and bundles of other options. They made recommendations we typically approved. As we learned, we changed to our own trading platform, one that was easy for beginners

> *and offered lots of helpful tools. Instead of money for set fees going to that oversight firm, it is growing in our portfolio. We are not saying this is the best choice for everyone. It works for us.*

Financial literacy bonus! As mentioned, exchange-traded funds are growing in popularity. They are a "great to know" nugget. An exchange-traded fund (ETF) is a basket of securities that trade on an exchange, just like a stock. ETF share prices fluctuate all day as the ETF is bought and sold.[4] No person is picking. No one is deciding what the price should be; it just changes according to what the buying and selling patterns determine it is worth at the time. Costs are generally lower for ETFs than mutual funds.

For people who are buying a share or investing some money in an ETF, the price changes throughout the day as other people buy and sell their shares.

We are not suggesting you do a deep dive on ETFs at this time. But when you do, you will enjoy it! As you become more financially literate, it is good to recognize the concept is out there and growing in popularity. ETFs might be a part of your portfolio. Here is an example of an ETF.

SPY SPDR S&P 500 Trust ETF, an exchange-traded fund, is designed to track the S&P 500 stock market index. SPDR is an acronym for the Standard & Poor's Depositary Receipts. Given its diversification, it is sometimes seen as a "set it and forget it" stock. (We are not making a

recommendation, just offering a learning opportunity.)
Given its consistent 10–11% growth over recent years, this is
a good tool to explore and learn its benefits, risks, and
functions. Keep in mind that what goes up can also go down.

Whether you are now paying attention to a portfolio you have, or to your 401(k) or IRA, or you're ready to create a portfolio, let's look again at our stewardship example in Matthew 25. Two wise stewards doubled what they were given. One did not. "So I was afraid and went out and hid your gold in the ground. See, here is what belongs to you" (Matt. 25:25). Note that stewardship buster, the emotion of fear!

Yes, take time to learn. Have conversations with others. You do not have to disclose amounts, but ask what is serving them well. Evaluate, get wise counsel, and then act.

Look forward to hearing these words to the stewards who increased what they were given. "His master replied, 'Well done, good and faithful servant! You have been faithful with a few things; I will put you in charge of many things. Come and share your master's happiness!'" (Matt. 25:23).

THINKING IT OVER

We hope you have increased your knowledge of terms common in the investment world. We hope we have increased your desire to learn more as it specifically relates to you. As your knowledge grows, so will your confidence.

If you have only a bank account and possibly savings account, we hope we have provided food for thought for how to store assets for later, even retirement, at a greater return.

If you have an IRA or 401(k), we hope you have an appetite now to look at it regularly and learn from its growth. Making projections (which none of us can do with perfect foresight) will help you determine if having an additional portfolio is wise.

If you have a portfolio, we hope that you are motivated to learn. How is it behaving? Toddler, teenager, or adult, it is yours (on loan from God). We hope you take ownership as a wise steward. There are many types of investments you can have in a portfolio, like real estate, precious metals, commodities—so we have only scratched the surface. The key to understanding these things is just to get started. Keep learning and do not let the industry jargon intimidate you. Keep that dictionary app open while you are reading.

Are you ready for more? In addition to considering return potential, you can consider whether any given investment aligns with your faith. There is growing interest in biblically responsible investing. We encourage you to research this, and look to resources like the *Faith Driven Investor* content we mentioned.

We especially hope you embrace God's entrusting you with whatever you oversee with joy!

18

HOW TO PICK A FINANCIAL ADVISOR

Whoever gives heed to instruction prospers,
and blessed is the one who trusts in the Lord.

PROVERBS 16:20

PROVERBS IS A WISDOM-PACKED book in the Bible, full of good advice about money. "Listen to advice" (Prov. 19:20). "Plans are established by seeking advice" (Prov. 20:18).

We have encouraged you to have your own Board of Directors (chapter 2)—six wise people you have invited to your life's boardroom table to speak truth and wisdom to you. One of those is a person wise in finances. You are transparent about money and listen to their wisdom.

You may want to select a credentialed advisor to help you oversee funds, especially if your financial situation is complicated, and/or you desire more growth with what God has entrusted to you.

For most of us, that financial advisor impacts our stability, future living, and ability to be generous. That means, PICK CAREFULLY.

You may benefit from a Certified Financial Planner or a Registered Investment Advisor. We will describe four possible types here. Fee-based means the advice they give is not based on their selling you a product, but rather the tasks they do on your behalf. This is one type of advisor. Some are flat fee. Commission-only advisors are paid by commissions from financial investments bought and sold. Yet other fees are an annual percentage of assets they oversee.

Get references from friends and associates for good certified financial planners. Get recommendations based on their using that person over a period of time. Check their reputation. Or go to a quality organization such as Kingdom Advisors for the Certified Kingdom Advisor network to find a financial planner. Use vetting resources like brokercheck.org.

Be especially careful if considering a friend or relative. In fact, we typically advise against that. Loyalty and a sense of obligation can still be a strong pull, and, in some cases, that is not a bad thing. But in many cases, it may make us hang on with someone who does not have our interest at the forefront of their recommendation. This is both a relationship AND a business transaction. What will happen when it is better for you to do business with someone else? Can that family or friend relationship handle that? If you do go with a family member or friend, discuss that up front.

Interview at least three potential advisors.

MIRIAM SAYS . . .

I asked three different planners what they would do with a specific sum of money given my needs and goals. The proposed plans I received were important information in making my choice. They showed the amount of fees to go to that planner as well as that advisor's choices of equities, mutual funds, stocks, bonds, and more. This was more than good to know. This is essential for every wise steward to know.

When asking them to present a potential plan, pick a number in the ballpark of the amount you will put in your portfolio. Some require a minimum amount to be their client.

Here are questions we need to ask:

How, and how much are you paid? Are you paid a fee by me, or a commission paid by a company for selling its product, or a combination of both? If there is no fee, and you are having trouble discovering how they benefit from the transaction, ask, "What transaction has to occur before you get paid?"

Also ask: Are you a fiduciary? Fiduciaries must put their client's interests first, before their own. Brokers must select suitable investments for you. Some Certified Financial Planners are fiduciaries. What are their credentials? Because someone has knowledge of personal finance does not mean they are ethical or have integrity. Belonging to a religious organization does not guarantee those qualities either. Ask for names of clients with circumstances similar to yours that you can contact.

The head of one international organization of financial

advisors stated, "Nobody will watch out for your backside" and "Everyone wants to part you from your money." She has a "trust-no-one-until-they-earn-it" attitude. That is wise.

Okay, ladies, never commit to someone who talks down to you. Require that they get previous approval from you before moving money. Have they listened to you?

> **VALERIE SAYS . . .**
>
> *Mom, one person was trying to sell you an annuity, saying you needed a sure monthly income. You had previously told them you had a pension that provided that. He did not listen to you. That annuity would have been unnecessary and costly—big commission money in his pocket, not your bank account.*

A good advisor is one who listens to you. So much so that they could repeat back to you what your hopes and goals are for the future. They will make projections and offer you a good perspective on what your chances are of obtaining those financial goals, but remember, they cannot predict the future. An advisor can help to set you on a course of action or recommended actions to achieve those goals.

You should be checking in with them quarterly, at least twice a year. This does not have to be a full review. And you should be able to know the status of all of your holdings by logging in and checking on them yourselves. But there needs to be a meeting of minds regularly on strategy and risk tolerance. Your life can take various turns and changes where your strategy and risk tolerances change with them. You and your advisor should be in sync, and hopefully in agreement about those. Remember: they give advice, YOU make decisions. You do not have to buy or sell every stock or mutual fund they recommend. It is good to ask why they are choosing that one over another. You will learn along the way what their style is and they will learn yours. If you trust and respect their advice and style, it's a match. If not, move on. Just like having the right family doctor or home contractor, a good fit here is really important. It is a lot of work to find the right fit in an advisor, but they have an important role in guiding you along the way to excellence in stewardship, and finding a good one is worth the effort.

> Remember—they give advice, YOU make decisions.

Deciding on the advisor you will use does not mean you can "check out." This work is not a one-and-done thing. After you have carefully picked a wise advisor, determine where you will direct your money to go. In other words, what assets will you own? That is just the beginning. No one will watch your investments like you. It is a heart thing. You know it is all God's entrusted to you. He says grow it. Use it wisely, be generous.

> Just as you oversee assets of your home or vehicle
> —for repairs, additions, functionality—
> oversee your investments just as thoroughly.

Monitoring your investments, you see whether your goals are being met. Are you growth-oriented? Or a dividend investor?

Dividends grow too! Maybe you like a mixture of both. Keep your eye on the big picture, long-term, not today's gyrations. Keep your emotions in check. Stay diversified. Life's seasons change.

A financial advisor who was a match at one time may not be one to stay with as life changes. Investment companies change their fees. Usually they get higher, and those companies may become less competent or stagnate. Wise women managing money are loyal to God and His principles. Loyalty to an investment company is not a virtue. Like shopping for insurance for your belongings, you may need to change for what meets your needs.

We hope you use these tools to pick wise financial counselors and advisors. Becoming wise women managing money means we also keep our eye on the big picture. We delay gratification to put funds away for the future. It is satisfying. We need balance.

THINKING IT OVER

Consider times when you have utilized the right professionals: physician, surgeon, dentist, banker, etc. How was that experience compared with those with ill-fitting professionals? What makes it work? What does not?

Does the professional have time for you? Do they respect you? Do you respect them? Have others successfully worked with them over a long period of time? How was their performance for that person? Are they coming close to the return you can get by investing in the overall market? Are they matching your investments to your risk tolerance? Do they explain concepts and point you in the direction of further resources where you can learn more?

Setting mutual expectations and clear communication is key for working with any professional. This person can be a wise guide—that is the goal.

19

THE IMPORTANCE OF A WILL

LORD, you alone are my portion and my cup; you make my lot secure. The boundary lines have fallen for me in pleasant places; surely I have a delightful inheritance.

PSALM 16:5–6

YOU OFTEN HEAR US SAY, "Tell your money where to go, or it will take you places you don't want to go."

We are talking about wills today. Here is our new statement. After you leave this planet, "Tell your money where you want it to go, THROUGH A WILL or a trust, or it will go places that would have made you sad."

> A will is a legal declaration of a person's wishes regarding the disposal of his or her property or estate after death.

Let's define wills. A will is a legal declaration of a person's wishes regarding the disposal of his or her property or estate after death.

A person can also name guardians for their minor children in a will. A will is written, legally executed, and directs where you wish your estate to go. Wills are governed by each state, so the rules about what "properly executed" means can vary. In some states, you must have a will signed, dated, and signed by two witnesses. Other states have other requirements. A will is meant to be read in probate court, by a judge, and the wishes of the deceased interpreted with it.

We were surprised to learn that 60% of Americans do not have a will.[1] It is simple to make one, is a loving action to take for those that are here after us, and can help avoid so much chaos. What happens then, when you do NOT have a will? All assets go through probate court. That requires lawyers: at least three, a judge and a lawyer representing the court, another the deceased. They are paid first from your assets before going to a set formula decided in your state. Many times that formula is: nearest relative first, and then others after the lawyers and court costs. Items and money go to relatives—whether they are your favorites or not. Nothing goes to charity or church. We hope we have convinced you to create a will.

Can you create a will without a lawyer? Yes. You can also create a kitchen without a contractor or a plumber. But should you? Online tools like LegalZoom describe how to do it yourself. States often require witnesses to sign the will, sometimes two. They may also require that a notary public validate the signatures on the document you created. A good lawyer can help you assess what documents you will need, and they often will have an initial conversation for free. If you're questioning, do I really need a will? Here is who does NOT: a person who is single, and childless, and broke, and has no possessions, not even a bicycle. For most others, having one is a matter of good stewardship. Entrust what God has given you to those who will be blessed by those assets, and use them wisely, including your church and favorite charities.

We will stop here to make a shameless plug for giving through your will (or trust—next chapter) to your local church. If you are a Christ follower, and belong to a local church body, please consider the following: Giving is an act of worship. The Bible talks about giving from your increase. There may be increase in your estate that you have not given from for good reason. Like on a home that has appreciated in value, but you have not given on the increase, because you needed to live in it! You may also need to hold on to some wealth to provide for increasing health care expenses that come with aging. But that is no longer true when you are in heaven. Consider what would happen if you, and every other devoted member of your church, gave a tithe of their estate. Your church might never again have to have a capital campaign! They may have to look around for areas that need *expansion* in ministry!

It is our personal belief that all the money needed, for all the ministry we could ever do, is in the hands of believers— right now. What if we released some of God's resources back into His purposes—at a time when we are guaranteed to not even need them anymore? That is like low-hanging fruit!

But we are under grace, and God loves a cheerful giver. So we submit these ideas for your consideration, not as a guilt trip.

If you wonder if dying without a will creates mayhem, research Pablo Picasso. Without a will, it took six years to settle his estate, and cost $30 million of the estate. He had six heirs, who eventually received something. There were many more folks who died without a will, including Abraham Lincoln, himself a lawyer. Our point is simply that not having a will is costly and wasteful. It is bad stewardship.

It is essential if you have dependent, minor children to designate who will have guardianship of them. Otherwise, the court will appoint a guardian based on what they consider the best interests of the child are. The court is not obligated to take into account your faith. That is important for you to know.

It might be wise to designate one person as guardian of your children, and another to be guardian of funds and assets. That nurturing adult or couple might not be financially suited to oversee assets as well. We consider having a will when you have dependent children, a serious and important parental responsibility.

Why are we going into such detail on all this? Because death is devastating and creates waves of distress. It is loving to have a will that clearly directs your wishes. This should lessen disagreements and hostilities that can march in behind the hearse. We see this happen regularly.

One couple died unexpectedly. They had no will. They were the owners of a farm and had four adult children with families. Only one lived in that state on the farm. Imagine being those grieving siblings trying to figure out how to move forward with a functioning farm and none whom were farmers. Probate, a dreaded, lengthy wait (and weight) while grieving.

A will is a loving action to take for those that are here after us.

We have known families where relatives "remembered" in hindsight what that person had promised them. If it is not recorded, it will not happen. Families that can enjoy traditional gatherings and have fun together can descend into conflict and even no longer see or communicate with each other over what happens with Mom and Dad's stuff after they have gone.

When you make your will, consider the fallout of your decisions. Here is an example: if one of your adult children is unwise with money, consider leaving assets for them in a trust with defined release dates. Those wise with money might receive a lump sum. It is better to communicate your plans before time, rather than discovering family "surprises" when the will is executed.

Are these joyful discussions? They are possibly hard, as no one wants to talk about death. But consider the future of those people you love. How can we first honor God, and then promote peace after we have left the planet? One of the estate-planning attorneys I (Val) respect the most states it like this: "The best goal with leaving wealth is that your children would be 1.) content and 2.) productive."

One wise widower who had wealth and many children and grandchildren planned a meeting with his adult children and the professional overseer of his portfolio. All knew that the meeting would be about his directions for his wealth. Having the independent "outsider" there provided more than just expertise on assets. They had a connection for questions and all heard the same facts of the will. Ahead of time!

Our final word is that our trust is in the Lord. "LORD, you alone are my portion and my cup; you make my lot secure. The boundary lines have fallen for me in pleasant places; surely I have a delightful inheritance" (Ps. 16:5–6).

Our stuff, where it came from and where it is going is not the Big Thing in our lives. We plan, we trust, and focus on His goodness to us.

THINKING IT OVER: DO YOU NEED A WILL?

In some states, there is a dollar amount under which the estate does not have to go to probate. That means your total asset value is quite small. In our state, for 2021, that number was $100,000. So, consider what your total assets might be.

Another consideration is that some assets do not have to be governed by a will or trust. Those are things with named beneficiaries like life insurance policies, IRAs, 401(k)s, and bank accounts. But if this does not happen properly—you guessed it—back to probate. One pretty definitive question is this. Do you own a home? If you do, this might tip the scales toward having a trust, not just a will. More about that in the next chapter. This can get complex, and an attorney, licensed in your state, is the best one to guide you through the process.

If you do not have a will or trust, who will have to bear the brunt of that decision? Likely your heirs. Is that what you intend? Probably not. But "no action" is also a decision—with consequences.

Remember, creating a will is an act of love.

20

THE FUNCTION OF A TRUST

A good person leaves an inheritance for their children's children.

PROVERBS 13:22

OUR GREATEST GO-TO resource for becoming wise women managing money is the Bible. It is packed with time-tested truths! Work and earn, then spend. Save and be generous. Be diligent. Invest wisely. Plan ahead. Above all, depend on God for every aspect of your money plan. And that is just a bit of money wisdom from the Bible.

Scripture includes examples of passing on wealth to future generations. Typically that wealth was land. Things have changed—land is only one of the assets owned today. But the principle of passing on wealth to bless future generations is still true. Our Proverbs 13:22 verse shares the principle that a good person blesses their children, even their children's children.

A tool today that accomplishes this is the trust. Trusts have distinct advantages over wills. We will clarify those. There's a host of different kinds of trusts. We will not do a deep dive on them, but it is good to be familiar with two most common designations: revocable, meaning you can change it; and irrevocable, meaning you cannot change it.

Let's discuss the revocable living trust. There is good reason why this topic is coming along later in this book. It is an advanced topic in the wise money management process. A trust is a legal entity that helps us do just that. Here is how it generally works: The trust, rather than the individual, is holding assets so those assets avoid probate. As we stated in the chapter on wills, the individual designates where they want assets to go. Probate fees can be avoided. Trusts avoid probate completely and achieve a variety of additional goals. The trust owns assets that are held for the beneficiaries of the trust, and the trust is managed by the trustee.

> A will is a legal entity with assets held by an **individual**.
> A trust is a legal entity with assets held by the **trust**.

You may have heard about trusts in the context of the ultra-rich having them. But they are not just for the ultra-rich. It is a great stewardship move. At least take a look at having a trust and evaluate whether you should have one. For most folks, we start out with a total net worth that is low, or even negative with college debt. That mortgage that might be greater than the home's value. But over the years, as earnings are greater, savings and investments have time to grow, we may end up stewarding far more than we ever imagined we would. The Bible talks about gaining wealth little by little. To prepare for surplus, to prepare to distribute surplus after we die, and to provide that inheritance for our children and even grandchildren, a trust is a key tool to have.

This revocable living trust is the most common, and is usually created, but not fully funded until your death. It includes all your instructions for how you want your estate divided among your loved ones, and how each person's share or interest in the trust is managed, administered, and distributed. Revocable living trusts are easy to amend, or change, which is important because life seasons and circumstances change.

Think of trusts as a box or basket. You create this legal basket. It accomplishes nothing unless you put assets into the trust. What do you own? A home? The deed to that home goes into the trust. Bank account, portfolio, business, any assets of worth should go into the trust. You put them into the trust by moving their title into the trust. This can be a bit tedious, but it is so important.

You give directions as to where the assets in the trust will go at your death. It is easy to change and important as children become adults, no longer need guardians, marry, and sometimes divorce. Trusts are biblical. You are directing what God has loaned to you, to where you wish those assets to go. You might name your favorite charities and church as beneficiaries stating a percent or set amounts to go to them. Remember, you can tithe with your will or trust.

With your assets in a trust, you can make one change to the trust, and that can be applied to all of the assets in the trust. If you have a will and not a trust, and you want to change beneficiaries, you must go to each asset and change beneficiaries. Trusts simplify the process.

Another advantage to trusts is privacy. The contents do not need to become public information. They can reduce estate and gift taxes. Assets go where you direct them to go efficiently, without the costs and delays, and publicity of probate. They can provide creditor protection for your inheritance. Another important benefit is that you can designate guardianship for dependent children. With a will only, the court determines that person, but usually follows the will.

Most choose revocable trusts. Life gives us constant changes. With the irrevocable trust, the grantor cannot change the written terms and no longer controls or has access to those assets. You might ask why would a person want to do that? Irrevocable trusts can be, and this is yet a more advanced topic, a means to avoid capital gains and estate taxes.

We hope you have learned a bit here and are thinking about what tools can serve you best. What might be your next steps?

If you already have a trust, review it. It is recommended that you review every five years. After divorce, your assets are different. Different homes, cars, a new business, and life changes result in different titles and assets. Especially review after becoming a widow.

If you do not have a trust, you have options. There are online resources; however, it is difficult to get a match for your needs, and they are probably not thorough. We recommend that you go to a vetted lawyer who specializes in trusts (estate planning). And, as with any lawyer, you want to get their fee in writing and what they deliver for that fee.

Remember Proverbs 13:22: "A good person leaves an inheritance for their children's children." Trusts are a tool to do just that.

STORIES FROM REAL LIFE

So, we want to share a few stories about what we have seen go well with wills and trusts, and what we have seen go poorly.

Through Widow Connection, we have heard time and time again where a husband has died and there was no will, no trust, and/or no life insurance policy. This can leave the surviving spouse devastated, and unnecessarily so. Families argue and bicker when there are no clear instructions. Widows have had to move out of their homes due to financial loss. In some states, if there is no will, the home value is divided between spouse and children. Yes, Mom can have to move out of that home, and proceeds are divided between her and all children.

One family we know could never locate the will they believed their parents had created. It is almost a decade later and those siblings are still having problems dividing the estate.

Meanwhile, its value dwindles and dwindles. This is not good stewardship.

It is relatively easy to attain a life insurance policy, to make a will, even to make a trust. But it will take some work and diligence. And there will be cost involved.

One thing you can do immediately right now for no cost is to look at every account or item you have that asks you to name a beneficiary, and make sure that is done and up-to-date. On your checking account, savings account, life insurance, 401(k), 403(b), IRA, and Roth, update beneficiaries.

How is your home titled? If you are married, what will happen with your home if something happens to both of you?

Beware of "cheap" fixes. Here is an example of one: One lady did not want the cost of creating a trust, so she just listed her three children on the title of her home. This cost her very little, maybe under a hundred dollars to record. When she died, the children did receive the proceeds of the sale of that home. But they also had to pay ordinary income tax on the growth of the value of that home, from the day their mother bought it over twenty years before. That was over $10,000 in additional tax for each child. So the "savings" of creating a trust resulted in a five times the loss by each child in inheritance.

Some folks will spend more time researching a flat-screen TV than they will in planning excellent stewardship and provision for their family after death. That is not the way wise women manage money.

We applaud you for going through the paces of considering whether a trust is right for you. But our applause is not important. Future generations may not recognize your good stewardship either. But know this. God does. His words matter.

"Well done, good steward. Well done."

THINKING IT OVER

While there is no simple chart that includes all the nuances comparing wills and trusts, this comparison tool describes generally their differences.

Comparison of Wills and Trusts

	WILLS	TRUSTS
Which can avoid probate?	Probate judge validates	Avoids probate
Who holds the asset?	The individual	The trust
Public or private record	Public	Private
Who designates your executor/trustee?	You do	You do

Your time is well spent deciding what serves you well. We suggest that you start by making a list of what matters to you regarding passing on wealth to others. Should you decide a trust is right for you, your list will be a helpful guide through the process.

One great blessing of making that decision is peace of mind knowing where it is going. Contentment indeed.

SURPLUS MONEY? CAUTIONS!

Whoever can be trusted with very little
can also be trusted with much.

LUKE 16:10

For the Spirit God gave us does not make us timid,
but gives us power, love and self-discipline.

2 TIMOTHY 1:7

SURPLUS MONEY, SUDDEN WINDFALL? You may think, "That will never happen to me." Maybe not; maybe it already has. In America, we are experiencing the largest transfer of money in our history, a new phenomenon. From inheritances and divorce to insurance settlements, stock option payouts, and even the lottery, some women experience that sudden windfall.[1]

God clearly tells us to enjoy what He has provided. "God, who richly provides us with everything for our **enjoyment**" (1 Tim. 6:17b). Many imagine, even dream of what they would do if they had that extra one thousand, or one hundred thousand, or even millions—lottery-style.

Suddenly money offers choices. To list a few:

Ability to no longer work at your income-producing job.

Ability to give generously to causes you treasure.

Ability to help family members with education and experiences.

Think college with no debt.

Travel to explore; even immerse in another language.

Let's check the facts. If more money is a blessing, which it can be, why is there a psychological condition to describe it: Sudden Wealth Syndrome?

> "Psychological condition or an identity crisis in individuals who have become **suddenly wealthy**." "**Sudden Wealth Syndrome** is characterized by isolation from former friends, guilt over their change in circumstances, and extreme fear of losing their **money**."[2]

Suddenly money also offers these choices. To list a few:

Ability to hand out to "friends" to gain favor or popularity.
Ability to put on the blitz and glitz. Don't others do that?
Ability to hoard in fear of losing what we have.
Ability to gift, with expectations of what we want in return.

Everything that God gives us as a blessing can be turned negative in our scarred world. We have seen both. Let's consider how to pursue blessings and avoid possible negatives.

SUDDENLY MONEY, BLESSINGS-STYLE

Lindsey was twenty-five when she received a significant promotion. In her sales world, not only did bigger sales numbers matter in commissions, they often led to a move up to a higher position. Commissions put more money in her bank account. The promotion assured her a set base income greater than she had before.

Take No Action

Her first and very wise move was to take no action. New cars looked glitzy, even a better apartment. She remembered her grandfather advising her to never have a credit card. "If you can't pay cash, you can't afford it." While having no credit card would not work in her world, she remembered his words and the example he set. Her savings account grew as she spent time considering her options.

Looking back after five years in her sales supervisory role, she counts the benefit of her "hit the pause button" strategy. Lindsey was able to focus on growing in her leadership skills, taking advantage of mentoring, and enjoying peace of mind.

Rhonda became a widow at age thirty-eight. Her husband's sudden death devastated her world and that of her four young children. Fortunately, he had life insurance, not a great sum, but generous. Within that first year, while she was still sorting out her own grief and parenting alone, a "financial" friend approached her advising her to put that money in a fund the "friend" oversaw to "grow for her children's college expenses."

Rhonda took counsel from her friend on her Board of

Directors (see chapter 2). With the encouragement of this friend who had wisdom about financial matters, and who had Rhonda's best interests at heart, she listened. With a bit of research, she found that the recommended fund was costly with upfront and oversight fees. Rhonda politely told her financial "friend" "No, thank you."

She needed time to settle her own spending plan, discover what her family's real income would be, wisely having savings for at least six months.

Since some widows are poorer than when they were married, even a small insurance policy needs protecting as that new season of life unfolds.

Take Time to Contemplate Your Values

Money offers opportunity to be generous in new ways. Lindsey realized she valued helping others develop their skill level. She began to research philanthropic organizations that focused on those women. Finding one that was rated well, and gave opportunities for her to volunteer, she was able to be generous with both her means and her time. She delighted in adding miles on her not-so-new, but well-functioning car.

The word "discipline" comes to mind accompanying suddenly money. "For the Spirit God gave us does not make us timid, but gives us power, love and self-discipline" (2 Tim. 1:7).

One gift is "God confidence" that He has entrusted His resources to us and is able to guide us well. Do not be timid. He gives us power to think, research, and pray. This is always time well spent. Self-discipline includes denying that emotional leaning toward impulsive action. We practice the discipline of practicing good stewardship of our spending plan before—and after—the suddenly money.

SUDDENLY MONEY, NEGATIVE-STYLE

Financial advisors have noted that most people with sudden surplus money experience a strong emotional impact. They are so influenced by their emotional roller coaster that for many, most of the money is gone within two years. Over 70% of lottery winners are back to being broke after three to five years![3] Similarly, professional athletes become suddenly wealthy and most have a short window of earning at that level. Many have little in later years.

Lottery winners and professional athletes often have this in common: they do not have years of money management experience leading to the windfall.

Quick Action Before Setting a Wise Spending Plan

That strong emotional impact window is a high impact to any woman, especially the vulnerable widow. Keeping suddenly money out of anyone's knowledge while sorting out your action plan might not be possible. "What do others expect of me now? A celebrity lifestyle might look appealing. Friends and even family view me differently now. What to do? What to do?"

Twenty-one-year-old Catherine inherited a large sum of money on that birthday. While she did not broadcast the news, the word trickled out. New "friends" became more interested in spending time with her on campus. She remembered the source—her grandparents were Jewish and had escaped Germany for a life of freedom and hard work here. That memory was foundational. She created a slightly more generous spending plan for herself, a modest increase.

The pull to surround herself with new friends becoming popular in their limelight was tempting. Having been a shy academic, she could have stepped into that circle. Revisiting her family history strengthened her convictions to oversee her inheritance instead of overspending it. She did not become the "pick up the tab" person in a new circle of friends.

Do Not Listen to the Wrong People

We have witnessed some with new money giving the spending reins to a friend. Big mistake. Just because a person is a friend does not mean they have good money management skills. They have friends, too, who want in on the ride.

As we said in chapter 11, if you have a bit of extra money in your pocket, someone will notice. Their "ask" is likely to come. We know of an "innovative" nephew who convinced his lottery-winning uncle to invest in his fledgling company. The company failed. While the lost funds did not devastate the uncle's resources, the relationship was severed.

One need not scroll far through stories of lottery winners to find stories of lives destroyed and marriages ended. Greed in family, friends, and acquaintances surfaced. Google lottery winners who wished they'd never won. The list is long. One winner stated he wished he had torn up that ticket.[4]

Review the guidelines in chapter 11 of when, whether, and how to give or loan money. They apply here as well.

SUDDENLY MONEY, GENEROSITY-STYLE

After reading the last section, you may think, can wealth really be a blessing? Scripture reminds us, "God, who richly provides us with everything for our **enjoy**ment" (1 Tim. 6:17b). Wealth can be a source of great joy. Our joy comes from our "why." What can be accomplished with wealth?

Scripture also tells us that when we are good stewards of what God has entrusted to us, small or large amounts, He often gives us more (Matt. 25). We have seen increasing wealth go into hands of both those who stewarded it wisely and those who misused it greatly. What was the difference?

The turning point from wisdom to foolishness with money is where love is placed. Loving God first and His generosity brings wisdom. Turning to love that money or wealth more than God brings foolishness and evil. Whether a person or organization, even church or charity, watching a portfolio grow can become an idol. Be inspired by reading the story of Robert LeTourneau, a man who gained great wealth, gave generously, and impacts the world yet today.[5]

Generosity signals that what we have is not ours. With open hand, we give. Grasping tightly what is in our hand is evidence of greed and fear. With the opportunity to be more generous than before, we have options. What charitable organizations and ministries do you value? You might already know your church well, and how well they oversee donations for kingdom purposes. You might have other charities you support. It may be a great time to focus and really impact that church or organization, or a good time to broaden your vision, and consider additional philanthropic organizations.

Consider putting funds in a donor-advised fund. You have flexibility there and the ability to give anonymously with those.

> A donor-advised fund (DAF) is a charitable giving account, an irrevocable commitment to charity.

These DAFs vary, but have this in common. They can make recommendations for where to give, as well as grow and invest those funds in the meantime. They oversee funds at a fraction of the cost of private foundations. One tax advantage is that money put into the fund is not taxed. One can put in large amounts to be distributed in the future, yet get the tax benefit at the time of the gift.

VALERIE SAYS . . .

Donor-advised funds may be a good option for you. This giving vehicle established as a public charity is the fastest-growing charitable vehicle in America today. It allows donors to make a charitable contribution to the fund and receive an immediate tax deduction. The donor then recommends grants to their favorite charities from the fund immediately or over time. Here is an important consideration in choosing a donor-advised fund. Does that bank or financial institution support your values?

Many banks and other financial institutions can help you set up your own personal donor-advised fund. Look carefully at their costs and guidelines, and also whether the assets in that fund will grow at the rate you would like.

You might use an existing giving fund. National Christian Foundation is an example. It is an easy-to-create, flexible account for charitable giving and is a popular alternative to creating a private foundation. Advantages are they are able to accept companies, complex investments, real estate, and more and have the expertise to monetize those donations.

All donor-advised funds have an annual cost. Compare them to pick the right vehicle for you.

Before making decisions, you might read books like *The Millionaire Next Door*. Some people are happy, even happier, to live that simple lifestyle they had before wealth. Our culture elevates spending for bling, for attention, even to find one's identity and validation. Let's be clear. It is okay to be wealthy, and it is okay to enjoy God's blessings. It is a heart thing. But let your heart belong to God, and realize those resources are all His. You will not take them with you into eternity.

THINKING IT OVER

Revisit your Rating Your Values scale in chapter 9. Suddenly money may change those a bit as your resources have grown.

Questions to contemplate:

▶ Am I full of gratitude and generosity directed by God's principles?

▶ Are God's principles my guidelines for what I do with all I have?

"Consider how the wild flowers grow. They do not labor or spin. Yet I tell you, not even Solomon in all his splendor was dressed like one of these" (Luke 12:27).

King Solomon in all his wealth and splendor (and his wealth was unmatched by any other in his day) was ordinary compared to the extraordinary beauty of God's wildflowers.

Consider that as a Christ follower, you already have blessings and gifts greater than any money can buy. No inheritance, lottery, or earnings boost can match His gifts He has for you. "I know what it is to be in need, and I know what it is to have plenty. I have learned the secret of being **content** in any and every situation, whether well fed or hungry, whether living in plenty or in want" (Phil. 4:12).

An ideal aspiration with Suddenly Money is to leave your heart with God, and aim for the goal that you, and others you can bless, will be content and productive.

IRAs, ANNUITIES, AND ROTHS

In their hearts humans plan their course,
but the Lord *establishes their steps.*

PROVERBS 16:9

SCRIPTURE ESTABLISHES WELL that we should plan ahead. It also establishes that God knows exactly what is ahead. We do not. We trust Him, and keep moving forward! But it is likely that we will have to slow down at some point; that we will have a time in later years when our ability to work as long, and our income, might diminish. Let's look at tools that help.

Popular tools are IRAs, annuities, and Roths. While we have mentioned these in earlier chapters, let's dig deeper in order to determine which, if any, are the right tool for you.

TRADITIONAL IRAS

An *individual retirement account* (IRA) is a tax-advantaged investing tool that *individuals* use to earmark funds for *retirement* savings.

One major advantage of a traditional IRA is that you put money **before taxes** into that investment reducing your taxable income. Rules apply. You must start taking money from that account at age seventy-two, even if you do not need it. That age is subject to change and can be verified, and should be verified, as you near retirement. You are taxed on those withdrawals as income. The assumption is that your income and tax rate will be lower in those later years, so you will save overall tax dollars. Many companies offer these. You can save money this way as an individual, or may participate in a similar type of account such as a 401(k) or 403(b) with your employer, or as an employer. These types of savings accounts are popular perks for employees.

ROTH IRAS

Roth IRAs remain a vastly underutilized retirement savings and investment vehicle. Instead, most people tend to rely on a traditional IRA model. They may not realize that a Roth IRA can offer tax benefits, and access to funds. They are easy to use, and the benefits are too attractive to ignore.

They work a different way than the traditional IRA. A Roth IRA gives investors a "pay tax now, save taxes later" advantage. Unlike 401(k)s or traditional IRAs, with a Roth, you do not skip the tax on your income that goes in, but you pay no taxes on distributions when the money is taken out—including the growth your investment earned—when you reach retirement age.

At present, Roth IRA ccontributions are limited. The maximum amount workers could contribute to an individual Roth IRA in 2021 was $6,000 if they are younger than age fifty. Workers age fifty and older can add an extra $1,000 per year in "catch-up" contributions. If the Roth IRA is inside a 401(k), 403 (b), or employer system, the limit is set by that program limit.[1]

Now let's assume you save that $6,000 per year amount starting at age thirty, and you retire at age sixty-eight. If you were to earn a 7% average annual return, that $6,000 annual savings would grow from the $222,000 total you put in, to over $1 million. Wise move. And you withdraw it paying no taxes.

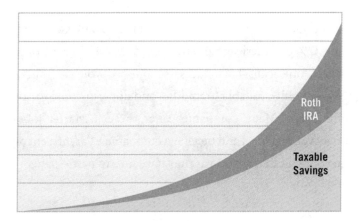

401(K)S

A 401(k) we referenced above is a qualified retirement plan that allows eligible employees of a company to save and invest for their own retirement on a tax deferred basis. Only an employer is allowed to sponsor a 401(k) for their employees. (At a nonprofit or government employer, it may be called a 403(b).) Your employer may also choose to match your contributions to the plan, and the majority do,[2] but this is optional for them.

If your employer offers that match, as we have said earlier, contribute and participate! It is free money!

Find out from your employer if you have access to a

401(k). Does that 401(k) go with you if you change companies? When do you "vest" (gain ownership and control) over the money? Can you choose the risk/reward aspect of that fund? Does it offer good investment options? Research and learn. There is much online that describes, defines, and helps you see whether this tool can serve you. We are surprised at the number of people who do not take advantage of these. Only 32% of Americans are investing in a 401(k); 59% of employed Americans have access to one.[3] If you are thinking these are only available to middle- and upper-income earners, think again. Many companies offer these in starter jobs— think even fast food and beverage companies. Parents, encourage your children as soon as they have jobs to participate.

ANNUITIES

Annuities are a tool where you give a lump sum of your money to an insurance company. In return, you get a guaranteed income stream the rest of your life, with a designated age for income to begin. Low risk, but high cost. Usually, on your death, money remaining goes to the insurance company.

In some annuities, if you die before you have received all of your money back, too bad for you. The insurance company keeps the money. In others, there may be an option for the money to go to a beneficiary.

In addition to the high cost, most annuity contracts charge stiff surrender penalties for early withdrawal, plus a 10% premature distribution penalty if you take withdrawals before age 59½. That 10% penalty is the same with many IRAs as well.

In some, you can include a beneficiary in the annuity contract so that the accumulated assets are not surrendered to the institution when the owner dies. The insurance company distributes the remaining payments to beneficiaries in a lump sum or stream of payments. It is true you do not pay taxes on an annuity during its growth phase. But when you start taking distributions, not only are you taxed, but the rate is higher than for many investments. Annuity gains are taxed as ordinary income, not as long-term capital gains.

Think of it this way: if life insurance is a defense against your life being too short, an annuity is a defense against you living too long (only meaning outliving your money). An annuity company would have lost its shirt on Methuselah!

Okay, ladies, this was lots of information. It is basic good stuff for all of us to be familiar with the terms, educate ourselves, and think of what works best in our situation. Knowledge is helpful, wisdom is precious, and being good stewards of all God has entrusted to us: priceless.

Notice we have not addressed the role Social Security or pensions might provide in later years. Predictions for Social Security continue to vary, but most consistently state that payouts will be smaller. Pensions for workers in the private sector are rare or minuscule. Public sector pensions (think government entities, like teachers, and local and state workers) vary in adequate funding.

Generally Social Security is not adequate to cover living expenses. Pensions, if you have one, may or may not. This statement bears repeating. Knowledge is helpful, wisdom is precious, and being good stewards of all God has entrusted to us: priceless.

A WORD OF CAUTION

Balance in planning for the future, versus living well today, can be a messy dance.

Stan and Sue in their early years of marriage came to a near-crisis in their marriage over their differences on saving versus spending. With two youngsters, and a home with few furnishings, Sue wanted a household budget that included some of her wish list. Stan had instituted an aggressive savings plan for college and retirement that required a tight budget in that season of life.

The road to agreement and accommodation was bumpy, including conflict and compromise. They weathered it and came eventually to benefit from their differences. They look back treasuring that they did take family vacations when their children were young. College days are yet ahead. They have some savings for that and will figure that out as well.

One couple in their forties (DINKs—double income, no kids) was advised by their financial planner to save a quite large amount of money (think millions) to continue their lifestyle in later years. They focused on work—think sixty hours a week at a minimum. In quite different lines of work, seldom did they have one day, even on weekends, to spend together. A health wake-up call got their attention. They put boundaries on their work hours, took walks together, got healthier, and enjoyed each other.

Proverbs 16:9 summarizes this well. "In their hearts humans

plan their course, but the LORD establishes their steps." Planning is good. We are each created differently. Whether single or married, our plans are not identical. No one else can make that plan for us, nor should they.

We plan as wisely as we can. And with comfort and contentment, put it in God's hands—which is where it belongs.

THINKING IT OVER

Considerations as you determine whether any of these tools are right for you include the following:

Pretax investment, or get taxed later. Pay tax now and invest, no taxes later. Which is the better match for you? You might have both types, especially if there is an employer/employee match. You might have to make an educated guess on whether you will have more taxable income now, or in retirement.

Some sources estimate that we need up to 85% of our pre-retirement income in retirement. We choose our lifestyle now, and we can choose it again then. Money goes where it is treated well. So can we in years when our income is lower. There is lots of information online comparing cities and states on their tax rates, property values, and even amenities including access to good healthcare. God has created us to be flexible creatures. Learn, take action, and trust. God notices and honors our heart.

DIRECTION THAT MATTER$

Coming to the final section of the book, we recognize that simply having good information on a host of financial topics might accomplish nothing. It is taking action that matters. In our two-generational approach, you see that we are different—our plans, our perspectives, and the actions we take.

We will take one chapter and discuss generational characteristics and challenges. It has been said that one thing we learn from history is that we don't learn from history. We reject that. We believe we can learn from generations before us, and younger ones as well. Not only do the discussions matter, actions seen have an impact.

MIRIAM SAYS . . .

I recall clearly the auction on our farm of all the farm implements at the time of our bankruptcy. It was spring of my senior year in high school. My mother had left home when I was thirteen to work, earn money, and save the farm. It did not work. As the president of our high school band, I was in charge of the fundraiser in our yard: selling donuts and coffee to the farmers at the auction. Smiling and selling, my heart was breaking. My favorite tractors, a Minneapolis Moline, and John Deere, sold for peanuts. I had driven them from the time I was twelve. Spending hours on these two friends in the hayfields, the smell of newly mown hay transformed the hot long hours working into a life-impacting treasure.

I saw much in those teen years that I did not want to repeat in my life. My mother returned after I left for college. We never talked about her decisions or why. I learned simply watching actions.

VALERIE SAYS . . .

Mom does frugality to an extreme, sometimes wearing shoes that are worn and embarrassing. But understanding where she came from, we give her grace. This is huge! She made sure that my three brothers and I were well dressed: soccer cleats, running shoes, Sunday shoes, and school shoes.

We toured the United States in a conversion van, often including another child, relative, or friend. We did not lack adventure or stories to tell, like sleeping in the van in Canada and waking up to ice around us. Actions matter. We were impacted by both our parents' frugality and generosity.

We hope the following chapters inspire conversations, and not just learning, but taking action.

GENERATIONAL CHARACTERISTICS AND CHALLENGES

Start children off on the way they should go,
and even when they are old they will not turn from it.

PROVERBS 22:6

SEASONS OF LIFE bring blessings and challenges. Millennials, Generation Xers, Baby Boomers, and now the youngest, Gen Z. Each has its blessings and challenges. Becoming wise women managing money, we acknowledge it, learn, and hopefully our generation passes a wise baton from one generation to the next. Proverbs 22:6 says train children early on the way they should go and they'll not turn from it when they are older. It can happen.

Let's get perspective. Proverbs are principles, not promises. Consider the prodigal son who blew his inheritance, and King David's children, whose lives were messy. Yet we can train, teach, model, and communicate. At least we can lay a foundation. Eli was a faithful priest, yet his sons Hophni and Phinehas were evil. We do not control the next generation, but we can offer them a good start.

> MIRIAM SAYS . . .
>
> *I speak for myself. My generation has not done such a great job. I am hoping that women in different seasons of life talk and listen to each other. Bob and I did take our family of six to a one-day finance seminar focusing on budgeting. Our example was solid. Discussions? Rare, if ever. We could have done better.*

We are hoping in this chapter to encourage intergenerational conversations, understanding, and mutual encouragement.

DIFFERENCES

Millennial women, mid-twenties to forty, are blessed to be earning more than most older women did at that same age.[1] They tend to be less collectors of stuff. That is a good thing. They have more diverse educational opportunities and more work choices than older women.

More women today choose to never marry. Thirty percent today remain single, and that number is still increasing.[2] Moms have more choices today to work.

> MIRIAM SAYS . . .
>
> *I was one of the few working moms as my children grew up. Seventy-two percent of moms work today outside the home.[3] Does this impact our wealth? Certainly.*

Gender-based roles for women's decision-making in their homes on finances have been dismantled. Just the fact that most married women work outside their homes some portion of their married life impacts the dynamic of financial decision-making. Our focus is not to determine the "why" here. We are simply acknowledging that fact. Likely causes include their bringing to the family table a paycheck, and their growing financial knowledge that comes with earning, seeing that paycheck in her name, what is taken out, and seeing where it is going. Given that the average age for women marrying is twenty-eight,[4] and the average age of widows is fifty-nine[5], it is not uncommon for women who marry to be single more years than married. Financial literacy is not only helpful, it is necessary.

Millennials carry more debt. One in five carrying debt do not expect to pay off that debt in their lifetime.[6] Our culture draws them to be self-focused, to acquire stuff and experiences using credit for immediate gratification. "Let no debt remain outstanding, except the continuing debt to love one another" (Rom. 13:8). Tough to follow when our culture encourages debt.

Generation X, or middle-agers, are blessed to be the most connected, educated, and sophisticated generation ever.[7] In the past, they have been accumulators, of housing and its contents, transportation, and experiences.

VALERIE SAYS . . .

It is easy for people in my stage of life to feel smashed and responsible for children, and parents, even extended family. We even over house and rescue others. We can give out too much,

> *or hoard for selfish reasons. It is easy to neglect self-care in this season and focus on everyone else.*

We both recognize that keeping a financial balance of what we need for living, what we can share without crippling another person's work ethic, and giving to kingdom work is a good thing, and tough to juggle. Our life experiences draw us to volunteer: school boards, sponsors and coaches of athletic and debate teams. We juggle this while most of us work full-time.

> MIRIAM SAYS . . .
>
> *Valerie and I have lived this contrast. From the time my four children were in grade school, I worked full-time as a public high school counselor. I drove them to sports events and much more. When Valerie's three boys were in grade school, she not only ran for their school board, but became the president. At the same time, she attended law school and completed her JD.*

Does all this impact our financial reality? For sure. As we said earlier, presence in the work force and level of education, including participation in a broader range of leadership experiences, is one reason that women oversee most of the wealth in the United States today.

A blessing of being a Generation Xer is that women show up in places outside Christian circles. We are much needed salt and light in our communities. We also become informed of broad needs of kingdom investment. Our generosity focus becomes broader.

What about us baby boomers? We vintage folks can be tempted to hoard, fearing health crisis or just habits of frugality beyond what matches our reality today. We even hang on to our stuff.

One family member recently acquired a fixer-upper home. An entire closet was packed with plastic bags. Rooms had only a path through boxes of stuff. Six dumpsters later, there was still work to be done. Yes, this is extreme, but over collecting and saving stuff you will never use, including junk, starts somewhere.

I have watched you, Mom, as you have loaded up to donate stuff you have not used. Parting with items can be hard. But think, how could this benefit someone else, meeting their need? Does that item bring you joy? Would a picture capture the memory rather than keeping that object?

Matthew 6:21 tells us, "Where your treasure is, there your heart will be also." Stuff requires care, time, and repairs. Investing in eternal treasures gets crowded out.

SIMILARITIES

Our "relative" circle now at our kitchen table includes all of the above and more—Gen Z teenage girls, young women our twenty something young men bring, and no toddlers at the moment. We see the value of talk times in broader circles. The twenty something women with us at the kitchen table are curious about our widow projects in developing countries. They see that "retirement" gives freedom to invest full-time in kingdom equity. They see that a law degree can promote generosity as well as provide income. We see their longing to make a difference, sorting out their passions and opportunities. We are encouraged. They will have the capability to be more generous. We do not doubt that they will be.

One is a teacher in New York of disadvantaged children who speak little English and lack provisions for school lunches and supplies. This resourceful young teacher seeks out clothing to bring, appropriate for all family members, not just her students. She finds bicycles, and more. Her aged car pulling up to their home is a welcome sight. Again, we are encouraged to see her making a difference with great creativity. She is an effective teacher for sure. It just may be that her efforts of generosity beyond her professional role will make an even greater impact than that educational impact.

Would you like to relate more to the millennial and Gen Z women in your circle? Go to hot yoga classes with them. Survive if possible. Read books together like Kim King's book *When Women Give*. Meet and talk, different ages, coffee and green tea. Multigenerational talk times are opportunities to pass the baton. You can learn what is new about their experience with money and what is still true from your generation. Coming alongside each other, we become wiser women managing money. Enter their world. We can learn from each other.

MIRIAM SAYS . . .

My grandmother, Hatie McCoy, told me of her friend who always cut off both ends of a ham before putting it in her pan to bake. Hatie asked why. She stated her mom had always done that to make the ham fit in her pan. "But," Hatie replied, "your pan has room for the whole ham." "Oh," said her friend. She never again threw away both ends of the ham.

Not only do women today have bigger pans, we have baking ovens, convection ovens, microwaves, and surely more will be invented.

We have more to give and that trend will continue. We have more ways to be wise and more tools available. Let's use them. Learning from others does not necessarily mean imitating them. We gather information and sort it wisely.

THINKING IT OVER

Every generation needs emergency savings. We have that in common. But the generations can differ on the importance of home ownership, car ownership, and more. (Val: I like hearing about how much vegetables cost when my mom grew up. That helps me understand her perspective now and appreciate all she has adapted to. But it's kind of scary when my sons tell me how much it costs to go on a date now.)

A useful activity for all generations is taking inventory. This is simply checking the physical inventory of what we possess. Businesses do so to measure their financial health. Is inventory being used, stolen, does it exist for a purpose?

For us as wise women managing money, is our inventory serving a good purpose? Millennials who move frequently must take inventory. They often make their move in a car or small trailer. Those of us who move less frequently still benefit from the exercise. Younger generations do not want our Christmas dinnerware and peacock feathers stuffed in an oversized oriental jar.

MIRIAM SAYS . . .

No, I am not kidding. I have those and more.

Taking inventory is a good exercise for all generations. There is great freedom in living lightly.

EIGHT HABITS OF WISE WOMEN MANAGING MONEY

*For where your **treasure** is, there your heart will be also.*

MATTHEW 6:21

WE HAVE EXPLORED TOGETHER, learned, prioritized, and changed as we have moved through these chapters on finances. We trust you have initiated some great beginnings. A challenge we acknowledge is that it is easier to fall back into old behaviors than spring forward into new and better patterns.

> Habit: a settled or regular tendency or practice

A wrap-up for this book would be incomplete if we did not address this tendency to revert, and offer a tool to help. We have created a list of eight habits of wise women managing money. While you have read entire chapters on each of these, our purpose here is that you have a condensed list. Regularly revisiting this list is accountability in action. Has an old habit, like those in our budget buster chapter, crept back in to mess with your spending plan?

Habits are hard to change. Some studies say that it takes anywhere from 18 to 254 days to form a new habit. This is no surprise. We are created differently. Time required for both brain and behavior to cooperate vary by person, and habit.

We will start with the list of 8, then elaborate on each with specific thoughts. Regularly revisit this list, take inventory of how you are doing. Make this a quarterly exercise. Yes, a new habit! A life disruption or just slipping back is better caught early and addressed, than ignored or even unnoticed.

8 HABITS OF WISE WOMEN MANAGING MONEY

1. We acknowledge all we have is God's on loan to us to steward.

2. We take responsibility for knowing our finances.

3. We create a spending plan based on our income and values.

4. We prioritize money management health as an indicator of our heart.

5. We do not make excuses about our finances.

6. We take personal responsibility for all financial actions.

7. We regularly revisit our spending plan and revise with wisdom.

8. We are generous for kingdom purposes.

1. *We acknowledge all we have is God's on loan to us to steward.* There is such power in knowing our "why." We acknowledge that all we have is God's on loan to steward wisely. It is biblical: over two thousand verses in Scripture refer to money, greed, wealth, ownership, and contentment.[1] It is motivational: God has entrusted us with what we "own." It is comforting: He will guide us, answer our prayers for direction. It is true: much in life changes. God and His word do not.

2. We take responsibility for knowing our finances.

This essential beginning means we know where our money is going, or is NOT going. How is that working out for us? Know it, own it, like it, or change it! Women have always made decisions regarding what is available and what needs to happen. We have entered a time where more women are overseeing, or at least can oversee. Time to KNOW.

3. We create a spending plan based on our income and values.

Earn **first** and then spend. Spend less than we earn. This is countercultural, for sure, in our easy-credit, grow-debt world. Calculating and recording is really easy. The discipline and work of shrinking spending so we can reach our goals? It is hard, but we can do it.

4. We prioritize money management health as an indicator of our heart.

Money does not necessarily change us or shape us; it just shows who we are. Health for our body, soul, mind, or spirit requires paying attention. We establish good habits, what we eat, how we exercise. This is true for healthy money habits as well. Just as a scale does not change us or shape us, that scale just reports the news. What do we weigh? Our spending plan, or lack thereof, is simply a report, a record of what is coming in and where it is going. This indicates our behavior, not our wish list. Our actions shout louder than our words.

5. We do not make excuses about our finances.

There is plenty of blame to go around. The economy tanked, wild spending spouse, irresponsible parents, needy kiddos, smooth-talking scammers. Knowledge is power, and God promises wisdom. No excuses necessary. We can be wise with the things that ARE within our control. Remember our speeding car example? If you are driving the car, you are expected to know the speed limits and abide by them. How hard is that? For that "foot heavy" driver, or one who sets the auto speed ten miles above the speed limit, consider deciding to go the speed limit only. It is hard. Everyone seems to be speeding past me! A conscious, long-term decision and action is required as that new habit is established.

After the Know It, comes the Own It.

6. We take personal responsibility for all financial actions.

It is not enough just to know where it is going, wise women following the Lord *direct* where it is going. What did God entrust to us? We report back to Him. Lord, here is the snapshot of my day/month/year. Wise stewards report back their positive outcome. Our spending plan, like that scale, simply reports the news. Progress is to be commended. God's commendation is priceless.

7. We regularly revisit our spending plan and revise with wisdom.

If you are a mom, you know the grocery budget when your first child came was hugely different from when you have three teenage, athletic three-sport sons.

MIRIAM SAYS . . .

We had four teenage drivers at one time. The budget stretch was a first-world problem. Think auto insurance with three of our teens being boys. Visiting what we value keeps us trimming some areas and expanding others. I asked my grandson what he thought people living in other countries thought of us as Americans. He replied, "The things we complain about, things we call our problems, they'd like to have them."

Wise words. He has been to Africa with us, and China, and seen a thing or two. Setting goals and revisiting your values? His words put our spending plan in perspective.

> "The things we complain about, things we call our problems: others might like to have them."

8. We are generous for kingdom purposes.

Why do we give? Because we are made in God's image (Gen. 1:26, 27). God is generous. He gives us life, He gave His Son for our eternal salvation, the air we breathe, everything we eat and drink. He continually gives. It is no surprise then, that when we give, we are happy—in fact, ecstatic. We are reflecting God's image. We feel that joy leaving a graduation of our widows' projects in Africa or Albania.

In addition to the joy of generosity, we have another blessing—the joy of relationship with those with whom we share. We have seen the need, whether it is life, adoption, healthcare, education, housing, or safety. The needs in this world are endless. We see, we are prompted.

When Jesus fed the 5,000 hungry listeners (actually, probably 20,000 counting women and children), He could have called down bread from heaven, or caviar and lobster. But He asked His disciples to find food. They did, though the boy's tiny lunch was no match for the multitude. In God's hands, it multiplied to feed them all and have leftovers. Imagine what that little boy told his mom that night! We imagine the disciples filled his lunch pouch with more fish and loaves than were packed in that morning. Maybe leftovers enough to feed his family for supper.

Jesus sees our actions and our hearts. He knows and responds. Treasures in heaven neither rust nor decay. Nor do they tank on economic hard news. Nor can they be stolen. Our wisest investments for sure.

THINKING IT OVER

What is your most effective reminder tool? Incorporate these eight habits into your reminder format. Some might put it in their calendar, a quarterly date to review the eight habits. You might not need reminders for all eight. Pick your hardest and use a more frequent prompter.

Getting an accountability partner gives you an encourager, a prompter, whether it's phone calls or emails, that touch point reminds us of our goals. Revisit your Board of Directors. Might your "board member" for finances be helpful? You might connect with your encourager as well.

We caution about revealing specific numbers. Individual values vary. Capabilities vary, and others' realities might be quite different. Yet seeking others' general input gives us more information, feedback to make informed decisions.

What bumper pads are others using that help them stay within their budget? It is not just financial health we are pursuing. We are pursuing following God's financial standard. We are pursuing the health of our heart for God.

KINGDOM EQUITY

For we are God's handiwork, created in Christ Jesus to do
good works, which God prepared in advance for us to do.

EPHESIANS 2:10

For you created my inmost being; you knit me together in my
mother's womb. I praise you because I am fearfully and wonderfully
made; your works are wonderful, I know that full well.
My frame was not hidden from you when I was made in the secret
place, when I was woven together in the depths of the earth.
Your eyes saw my unformed body; all the days ordained for me
were written in your book before one of them came to be.

PSALM 139:13–16

WE WOULD LIKE to introduce you to a new concept: Kingdom
Equity. The word "equity" usually refers to the value of something. We have been talking about money and other valuables
God has entrusted to our keeping. We understand the concept
of equity as it relates to finances. A common usage is home
equity, referring to the value that you actually own in your
home. Equity in our home is value; in investments, it is the

worth of that holding. Equity is a good thing to have. We think of equity as money.

This concept, Kingdom Equity, is bigger, broader, and more inclusive. Also, it is quite relevant for us as women growing in investing what God has entrusted to us.

MIRIAM SAYS . . .

I was introduced to this concept in a most unique way. A stranger approached me after I had made a presentation to a hospital staff in Lilongwe, Malawi. "Miriam Neff," he declared, "you are rich in Kingdom Equity."

I was more than puzzled; I was intrigued. I know a bit about equity, but had never heard of Kingdom Equity.

I asked if we could talk a bit more after I had greeted the departing staff. We did.

We found a quiet corner where he introduced himself and explained what had brought him to Africa. He already had heard my story and knew the work I was doing there. We train widows in a self-sustaining skill, often tailoring.

He told me that Kingdom Equity is God's investment in me. Our Creator God is building a good place for us, His kingdom, called heaven. The kingdom also refers to good places and good things here on this earth. God desires our best in this kingdom, as well as heaven ahead. He wants us to contribute to what He is building on earth that will last forever, making it better for others.

Drawing on what I had shared that motivated and

equipped me for my work in Africa, he began to describe what he saw as God's equity building in my life:

- A farm girl learning to sew on a treadle Singer sewing machine. (God knew I would need that later.)
- A farm girl living temporarily in a home with no indoor plumbing. (Also needed in Africa.)
- World travels that left me hungry for more planet-roaming experiences.
- A courageous attitude, "Let's get at it" spirit. Or, as my husband described it, my absence of a "fear chip."

He continued the list from the little he knew of me in that one meeting.

I rapidly took notes, recognizing that I wanted to add to his list. This new perspective cast a different and valuable light on seemingly ordinary things, even hardships. I began to see things in my past that had current Kingdom Equity value.

At the age of ten, my childhood home was destroyed by fire. Investment: I recognized treasures here are temporary— added Kingdom Equity in my life. Living lightly is a blessing and freedom indeed.

Kingdom Equity: Life experiences, whether positive or negative, GIFT you with wisdom, experience, information, and faith. Everything in your life is a part of God building valuable equity in your life.

VALERIE SAYS . . .

Kingdom Equity is a precious concept that pieces together what we often see as random things in our past and present circumstances. But they are not random. God is investing in us intentionally. He is building Kingdom Equity. Seemingly throwaway skills might be on the list as well as important earned degrees. When I was still working very part-time, and was mostly an "at home" mom, I served on a few boards, even was president of two of them. Leading boards and knowing "Robert's Rules," which govern boards, seemed like very random skills to learn at the time, but these lessons have proven so valuable as I have returned to the workforce.

MIRIAM SAYS . . .

I have no idea how long that conversation lasted in Malawi. It seemed too brief. We both had to move on to our next commitments.

Under my mosquito net that night with a feeble bedside lamp, I was grateful that the sporadic electricity stayed on. I scribbled as long as my tired body would allow. College degrees were on the list, but were not the significant standout equities. That "degree" in treadle sewing with Professor Grandma Hatie and her eight-year-old student had a value I had not treasured before.

I looked again at my scribbled notes from our conversation. My final entry at the end of my Kingdom Equity list, quoting his words, read: "You've Got It, Miriam, Now Spend It."

We have a challenge for you. We have always said, all you have is God's on loan to you to steward wisely, assets, everything. Let's look at the broader picture. "For we are God's handiwork, created in Christ Jesus to do good works, which God prepared in advance for us to do" (Eph. 2:10).

Your experiences whether hard, simple, forgotten, life shaping, even life-threatening are His investment in you. There are no throwaway moments or years. Everything can be used for God's glory. Even things that others meant for evil. God can turn that into good. May we never forget that He still does the miraculous. Read about the life of Joseph considering this concept, and know that his same God is yours.

THINKING IT OVER

We encourage you to make your list, threads from your past, skills, training, people, places. Hopefully, you will not have to do so under a mosquito net with a dim bedside lamp that flickers. Lay your life experiences out before God with all your other assets. And thank Him first. "Lord you have invested in ME."

Next question: What now, Lord? This Kingdom Equity —we have it, now spend it.

LEGACY GIVING:
GIFTS THAT MATTER

*On the first day of every week, each one of you should
set aside a sum of money in keeping with your income.*

1 CORINTHIANS 16:2

It is more blessed to give than receive.

ACTS 20:35

WE STARTED THIS BOOK together on becoming wise women
managing money, thinking together about what matters.
Women already control over 51% of our nation's wealth and
that percent is rising rapidly.[1] We know that the love of money
is a powerful thing. It can control us, not us control it, if we
let it. Thankfully Scripture is full of wisdom, guidelines, and
examples of how to view and handle money. All resources are
God's on loan to us. How DO we steward them wisely?

We have talked about spending plans, budget busters, and
investing. Let's step back and look at the bigger picture. Or
maybe we should say look up from the dailies of life at what
matters—**really**. Let's talk generosity and legacy.

What are we giving to others? It is not just money; it is time, a sense of belonging to family, a legacy of faith, love, and respect. We can give others an understanding of who God is, about how He speaks to us in the Bible, and a demonstration of wise stewardship. What we give, and how we give it, reflects our heart, what matters.

Women are generous. In the past, women have had fewer resources but have given larger portions of their wealth to charity.[2] Women today have a greater range of interests, more education, and more varied experiences than before. Work experiences are changing from supportive positions to leadership and entrepreneurship. God is entrusting us with investments for the kingdom.

Let's look at how women in Scripture gave. A popular saying is: "Do your giving while you're living so you're knowing where it's going." In other words, give with a warm hand. Here are two women in Scripture who did just that.

Mary, the sister of Martha and Lazarus, anointed the Lord with perfume and dried His feet with her hair (John 11:2). She repeated this again shortly before His death (John 12:3). Each jar of that perfume was worth a year's wages, possibly her life savings.

What she gave revealed her heart. More important than her dowry, which that perfume might have been saved for, was her love for Jesus. It was an act of love and worship.

Luke 21:1–4 tells the story of the poor widow who gave two small coins. And it adds that Jesus tells His disciples: "'Truly I tell you,' he said, 'this poor widow has put in more than all the others. All these people gave their gifts out of their wealth; but she out of her poverty put in all she had to live on.'"

I write about her in my book Not Alone. *We do not know her name, but Jesus does. She is forever memorialized in the Bible and highlighted by Jesus Himself. She is still an example of generosity to millions yet today.*

Be encouraged that these two examples are extreme opposites as relates to worth. Mary's was at least a year's wages. Think of your annual income, a 100% gift. Two mites would have been a small fraction of a day's wages. And this widow was on her own, no backup plan. Not really, she was trusting God. Both women were highly commended by Jesus, though the amounts they gave were immensely different. Quite large, quite small, equally commended.

We hope we have made the case for generosity as an essential part of being a wise woman managing money. That includes the here and now, and after you are in heaven. We urge you to become a woman who both wants to be more generous, and who has the capacity and a plan to make it so.

One study of over 7,000 women revealed that they could give more, but they did not have a clear understanding of their purpose or passion. They also wanted more teaching on the biblical principles of giving.[3]

There are many biblical principles about giving. The Bible is pretty clear about giving to your church. It is also pretty clear about caring for the poor, orphans, and widows. "Religion that God our Father accepts as pure and faultless is this: to look after orphans and widows in their distress and to keep oneself from being polluted by the world" (James 1:27). We want to care about the things God cares about. And He does talk about marginalized people in the Bible.

Here is another one of those biblical principles: Scripture says bless your children and grandchildren. "A good person leaves an inheritance for their children's children" (Prov. 13:22). This can be with an inheritance, which we have discussed in chapters 19 and 20 on wills and trusts.

In the here and now, if you have wealth to give and assessed you have a surplus (meaning have ascertained you have a surplus over and above funds that are already spoken for), in addition to a good financial plan and projection that you can meet your financial needs as long as you are alive, you have an option to give $15,000 each year to a relative (actually to anyone) with no tax paid. If you are married, $15,000 from each of you. That is $30,000 a year. You can see how those folks spend it. Now you have wisdom gained about what they might do with an inheritance.

Consider anonymous giving. Giving for the sheer joy of blessing that person, church, or organization. That gift removes any temptation of expecting anything in return. Our human nature wants to be charitable with some recognition. Religious leaders in Jesus' day were no different. Matthew 23 warns us not to be like they were, seeking personal recognition.

We want giving to be all about honoring God and blessing

others. We see needs through our eyes. Each of us are created in His image, planned and uniquely designed since conception. God has made us as individuals with different capacities for giving and different passions for where to give. What prompts your passion?

MIRIAM SAYS . . .

You know mine: Empowering abandoned women and widows to be self-sufficient. We want them to know God and be able to care for their children.

Give your time to a purpose you care about. Tutor children, provide legal service to those who are voiceless. Combat homelessness, human trafficking. You can teach and promote kingdom purposes, break the cycle of poverty. Volunteer at your church.

Meet with a group of friends. With a whiteboard, write what skills, talents, interests each of you have. Your friend might see a strength in you that you have not noticed before.

Take that first step to investigate: who is doing this in my area? Can I come alongside them with time, talents, and funding? Christ followers are needed in so many areas.

MIRIAM SAYS . . .

Valerie, you ran for your local school board, won, and became the president. Donated talent.

Each of us will leave a legacy. Our desire, and our prayer for each of you who have joined us, is that your legacy is bigger than what matters to you. Your legacy shines a light on what matters to God. You can pass along a propensity for generosity. It has been said that children absorb more by observing our actions and example, than by what we say. You might want to involve children and grandchildren by helping them learn to be generous. Give them money to give away so they can start researching charities and see what they are passionate about supporting. You may eventually want to move to matching their generosity so they have "skin in the game" and are taking ownership and are personally invested in the cause, organization, or church they support.

May our legacy, our mark, be positive. Salt, preservatives of good, and lights in this world reflecting God's heart (Matt. 5:13,14).

THINKING IT OVER

Here are a few of our favorite generosity ideas: Gift money for children and grandchildren to give away. Make their explanation of why they chose the place to give the money to a part of your holiday celebration. You will learn things you never knew about your family.

Be a really good tipper. Carry around some cash so that you can take advantage of an opportunity to bless someone. You can do this anonymously or not. Just doing this with humility and gratitude to the Lord for the chance to do so, can be a blessing.

Be quick and genuine to compliment someone who is doing a great job. Be on the lookout to spot people who are doing good things and performing a job well done. Many times they are doing that job or service in the face of great difficulty, especially in these years. This kind of tipping is free! We can be generous with money, and in spirit.

At work, or in business, carve out time and attention to help someone professionally who cannot help you professionally. Mentor. Share wisdom. Take a personal interest in the success and development of someone else. Maybe do this for someone who would not normally be on your radar. Introduce others to professional connections, especially if they are just starting out, out of work, reentering the workforce from staying at home rearing children, or in a disadvantaged position.

When climbing the corporate or professional "ladder," it is not enough just to not step on others as a ladder rung. Purposefully turn around and lend a hand to others a step or two behind you in the climb.

Let a car go ahead of you, even if you have the right of way. Let a large truck go past you without cutting them off. Open the door for someone else, even when you got to it first. The list goes on . . .

Are you bored and need a hobby? Shock others with your generosity. Discover ways to be anonymously, radically generous. The Bible even says that when we are generous, we cause others to praise the Lord. "I made the widow's heart sing" (Job 29:13).

One of the amazing and unexpected things about embracing a life of generosity is that it produces great joy. Bring your own creativity into the generosity process and be open to God's promptings. If you have followed the steps to be wise in managing money, it will likely follow that you will have financial margin to be generous. Go for it!

ACKNOWLEDGMENTS

Our thanks to Jennifer Graham and Jennifer Tinapple who helped bring this project into being.

Many thanks to Ruth Guillaume, who has mentored many in biblical finances and generosity.

Thank you Mark Hogan for encouraging and supporting us to pursue the ministry work the Lord has for us in writing this book.

NOTES

Chapter 1: What Matters: Know It, Own It, Like It, Change It

1. Karen DeMasters, "Women Hold Majority of Personal Wealth, but Still Minorities in Advisory Field," *Financial Advisor*, March 25, 2020, https://www.fa-mag.com/news/women-need-to-lead-in-finances-consultant-says-54850.html.
2. "Unmarried and Single Americans Week: September 20–26, 2020," United States Census Bureau, September 10, 2020, https://www.census.gov/newsroom/stories/unmarried-single-americans-week.html.
3. Krystal Barker Buissereth, "How to Plan for the Unique Financial Challenges Women Face," MarketWatch, March 23, 2020, https://www.marketwatch.com/story/how-to-plan-for-the-unique-financial-challenges-women-face-2020-03-23.
4. Hannah Wright, "Women's Wealth: 75% Lack Financial Confidence, Survey Finds," Private Banker International, November 17, 2020, https://www.privatebankerinternational.com/news/womens-wealth-75-lack-financial-confidence-survey-finds/.

Chapter 4: Credit Cards

1. Bill Hardekopf, "Do People Really Spend More With Credit Cards?," *Forbes* magazine, December 16, 2020, https://www.forbes.com/sites/billhardekopf/2018/07/16/do-people-really-spend-more-with-credit-cards/?sh=3cef51b21c19.
2. Erin Hurd, "Credit Cards Can Make You Spend More, but It's Not the Full Story," NerdWallet, July 27, 2020, https://www.nerdwallet.com/article/credit-cards/credit-cards-make-you-spend-more.
3. Clint Proctor, "What Credit Score Is Needed to Buy a House? It Depends on Your Lender and Loan Type," Business Insider, October 21, 2020, https://www.businessinsider.com/personal-finance/what-credit-score-is-needed-to-buy-a-house.
4. Aimee Picchi, "Here's a Top Reason Americans Are Carrying an Average Credit Card Balance of over $6,200," *USA Today*, February 12, 2020, https://www.usatoday.com/story/money/2020/02/12/credit-card-debt-average-balance-hits-6-200-and-limit-31-000/4722897002/.
5. "What Is a Credit Score?," Equifax, accessed January 6, 2021, https://www.equifax.com/personal/education/credit/score/what-is-a-credit-score/.

Chapter 5: Wise Women: Where to Store Assets

1. Anna Zakrzewski, Kedra Newsom, Michael Kahlich, Maximilian Klein, Andrea Real Mattar, and Stephan Knobel, "Managing the Next Decade of Women's Wealth," BCG, September 18, 2020, https://www.bcg.com/publications/2020/managing-next-decade-women-wealth.

2. Karen DeMasters, "Women Hold Majority of Personal Wealth, but Still Minorities in Advisory Field," *Financial Advisor*, March 25, 2020, https://www.fa-mag.com/news/women-need-to-lead-in-finances--consultant-says-54850.html.

3. Daniel M. Choi, "Council Post: Five Reasons Women Are Taking the Lead in Financial Planning," *Forbes* magazine, October 4, 2017, https://www.forbes.com/sites/forbesfinancecouncil/2017/08/08/five-reasons-women-are-taking-the-lead-in-financial-planning/?sh=142d9bc93500.

4. Bruce DeBoskey, "Women's Voices Ring Clear in Philanthropic World," Wealth Management, October 16, 2017, https://www.wealthmanagement.com/philanthropy/women-s-voices-ring-clear-philanthropic-world.

5. "Unmarried and Single Americans Week: September 20–26, 2020," United States Census Bureau, September 10, 2020, https://www.census.gov/newsroom/stories/unmarried-single-americans-week.html.

6. Tim McMahon, "Average Annual Inflation Rates by Decade," InflationData.com, January 1, 2021, https://inflationdata.com/Inflation/Inflation/DecadeInflation.asp.

7. Liz Knueven, "The Average Stock Market Return over the Past 10 Years," Business Insider, August 24, 2020, https://www.businessinsider.com/personal-finance/average-stock-market-return.

8. Will Kenton, "S&P 500 Index," Investopedia, December 22, 2020, https://www.investopedia.com/terms/s/sp500.asp.

9. J. B. Maverick, "What Is the Average Annual Return for the S&P 500?," Investopedia, February 19, 2020, https://www.investopedia.com/ask/answers/042415/what-average-annual-return-sp-500.asp.

10. *Collins English Dictionary*, s.v. "NASDAQ," accessed January 15, 2021, https://www.collinsdictionary.com/us/dictionary/english/nasdaq.

11. James Chen, "Russell 2000 Index Definition," Investopedia, June 17, 2020, https://www.investopedia.com/terms/r/russell2000.asp.

12 "Women of Wealth Study 2012," Family Wealth Advisors Council, accessed January 6, 2021, http://familywealthadvisorscouncil.com/women-of-wealth-study/.

Chapter 6: Housing

1. Camilo Maldonado, "Here Are 7 Common Myths of Homeownership and the Truth behind Them," *Forbes* magazine, December 15, 2020, https://www.forbes.com/sites/camilomaldonado/2019/03/21/7-common-myths-homeownership/?sh=479e5ef33d2f.

Chapter 8: Managing Debt

1. "U.S. National Debt Clock: Real Time," accessed January 11, 2021, https://www.usdebtclock.org/.

2. Dan Albright, "Average American Household Debt in 2020: Facts and Figures," The Ascent, The Motley Fool, November 18, 2020, https://www.fool.com/the-ascent/research/average-american-household-debt/.

3. "Income and Poverty in the United States: 2019," United States Census Bureau, September 15, 2020, https://www.census.gov/library/publications/2020/demo/p60-270.html.

4. Richard Fry, "Young Adult Households Are Earning More Than Most Older Americans Did at the Same Age," Pew Research Center, December 11, 2018, https://www.pewresearch.org/fact-tank/2018/12/11/young-adult-households-are-earning-more-than-most-older-americans-did-at-the-same-age/.

Chapter 9: Discretionary: Clothes, Food, Entertainment

1. Krystal Barker Buissereth, "How to Plan for the Unique Financial Challenges Women Face," MarketWatch, March 23, 2020, https://www.marketwatch.com/story/how-to-plan-for-the-unique-financial-challenges-women-face-2020-03-23.

2. "Women of Wealth Study 2012," Family Wealth Advisors Council, accessed January 6, 2021, http://familywealthadvisorscouncil.com/women-of-wealth-study/.

Chapter 10: Insurance

1. Jean Chatzky, "How Women Can Plan for Outliving Their Husbands," The Balance, updated March 14, 2019, https://web.archive.org/web/20200513040359/https://www.thebalance.com/retirement-plan-for-women-outliving-husbands-4139845.

Chapter 11: Loaning Money, Cosigning Contracts

1. Kendall Little, "Survey: Nearly Half of Americans Who Lend Cash to Loved Ones Face Negative Consequences," Bankrate, September 26, 2019, https://www.bankrate.com/finance/credit-cards/lending-money-survey-2019/.

2. Hannah Rounds, "Family Loans: What to Know Before You Borrow or Lend within the Clan," Credit Karma, December 19, 2020, https://www.creditkarma.com/personal-loans/i/family-loans.

Chapter 12: Marriage and Money

1. Elizabeth Cole, "Money Ruining Marriages in America: A Ramsey Solutions Study," daveramsey.com, February 7, 2018, https://www.daveramsey.com/pr/money-ruining-marriages-in-america.

2. Mark Banschick, "The High Failure Rate of Second and Third Marriages," Psychology Today, February 6, 2012, https://www.psychologytoday.com/us/blog/the-intelligent-divorce/201202/the-high-failure-rate-second-and-third-marriages.

3. Thomas Leopold, "Gender Differences in the Consequences of Divorce: A Study of Multiple Outcomes," NCBI, April 13, 2018, https://www.ncbi.nlm.nih.gov/pmc/articles/PMC5992251/.

Chapter 13: Emotions: Budget Busters

1. Russ Wiles, "Don't Let Financial Worries Cut Your Workplace Productivity," azcentral.com, August 24, 2017, https://www.azcentral.com/story/money/business/consumers/2017/08/24/russ-wiles-financial-worries-other-stresses-cut-workplace-productivity-study-says/578388001/.

2. Maurie Backman, "Your 3 Biggest Financial Fears—and How to Avoid Them," CNN Money, August 17, 2017, https://money.cnn.com/2017/08/17/pf/financial-fears/index.html.

3. Chris Gaetano, "Survey: 77 Percent of Americans Stressed Over Finances," NYSSCPA, January 28, 2020, https://www.nysscpa.org/news/publications/nextgen/nextgen-article/survey-77-percent-of-americans-stressed-over-finances-012820.

4. Elizabeth Cole, "Money Ruining Marriages in America: A Ramsey Solutions Study," daveramsey.com, February 7, 2018, https://www.daveramsey.com/pr/money-ruining-marriages-in-america.

Chapter 15: Danger! Filling Our Void with "Stuff" or People

1. "Americans Have Too Many Things and Not Enough Money, Study Finds," OfferUp, August 29, 2016, https://www.prnewswire.com/news-releases/americans-have-too-many-things-and-not-enough-money-study-finds-300319019.html.

2. Alexander Harris, "U.S. Self-Storage Industry Statistics," SpareFoot, January 27, 2021, https://www.sparefoot.com/self-storage/news/1432-self-storage-industry-statistics/.

Chapter 16: Crisis Equals Opportunity

1. W. E. Vine, *Vines Expository Dictionary for New Testament Words* (McClean, VA: MacDonald Publishing, 1989), 472–73.

Chapter 17: Knowledge, Goals, Risk Tolerance

1. J. B. Maverick, "What Is the Average Annual Return for the S&P 500?" Investopedia, August 26, 2020, https://www.investopedia.com/ask/answers/042415/what-average-annual-return-sp-500.asp.

2. Arielle O'Shea, and Tiffany Lam-Balfour, "What Is a Dividend and How Do They Work?," NerdWallet, February 11, 2021, https://www.nerdwallet.com/article/investing/what-are-dividends.

3. Jason Fernando, "What Is a 401(k) Plan?" Investopedia, February 17, 2021. https://www.investopedia.com/terms/1/401kplan.asp.

4. James Chen, "Exchange Traded Fund – ETFs," Investopedia, February 19, 2021, https://www.investopedia.com/terms/e/etf.asp.

Chapter 19: The Importance of a Will

1. "Nearly 60% of Americans Don't Have Wills," InvestmentNews, February 6, 2017, https://www.investmentnews.com/nearly-60-of-americans-dont-have-wills-70548.

Chapter 21: Surplus Money? Cautions!

1. E. Napoletano, "8 Tips for Managing a Financial Windfall," *Forbes* magazine, April 26, 2020, https://www.forbes.com/advisor/personal-finance/tips-for-managing-a-financial-windfall/.

2. James Chen, "Sudden Wealth Syndrome (SWS)," Investopedia, reviewed on August 8, 2020, https://www.investopedia.com/terms/s/suddenwealthsyndrome.asp, emphasis added.

3. George Loewenstein, "Five Myths about the Lottery," *Washington Post*, December 27, 2019, https://www.washingtonpost.com/outlook/five-myths/five-myths-about-the-lottery/2019/12/27/742b9662-2664-11ea-ad73-2fd294520e97_story.html.

4. Melissa Chan, "Powerball: How Winning the Lottery Makes You Miserable," *Time*, January 12, 2016, https://time.com/4176128/powerball-jackpot-lottery-winners/.

5. See R. G. LeTourneau, *Movers of Men and Mountains* (Chicago: Moody Publishers, 1967).

Chapter 22: IRAs, Annuities, and Roths

1. "Retirement Topics—IRA Contribution Limits," Internal Revenue Service, accessed February 28, 2021, https://www.irs.gov/retirement-plans/plan-participant-employee/retirement-topics-ira-contribution-limits.

2. Roger A. Young, "4 Reasons 401(k) Plans Still Make Sense," Kiplinger, August 25, 2020, https://www.kiplinger.com/retirement/retirement-plans/401ks/601299/4-reasons-401k-plans-still-make-sense#:~:text=Taking%20advantage%20of%20an%20employer's,plus%2076%25%20of%20smaller%20plans.

3. Paul Deer, "The Average 401k Balance by Age," Personal Capital, *Daily Capital* (blog), August 6, 2021, https://www.personalcapital.com/blog/retirement-planning/average-401k-balance-age/.

Chapter 23: Generational Characteristics and Challenges

1. Richard Fry, "Millennial Households Are Earning More than Most Older Americans Did at the Same Age," Pew Research Center, December 11, 2018, https://www.pewresearch.org/fact-tank/2018/12/11/young-adult-households-are-earning-more-than-most-older-americans-did-at-the-same-age/.

2. USAFacts, "The State of American Households: Smaller, More Diverse and Unmarried," U.S. News & World Report, February 14, 2020, https://www.usnews.com/news/elections/articles/2020-02-14 the-state-of-american-households-smaller-more-diverse-and-unmarried.

3. Juliana Menasce Horowitz, "Despite Challenges at Home and Work, Most Working Moms and Dads Say Being Employed Is What's Best for Them," Pew Research Center, September 12, 2019, https://www.pewresearch.org/fact-tank/2019/09/12/despite-challenges-at-home-and-work-most-working-moms-and-dads-say-being-employed-is-whats-best-for-them/.

3. Amanda Barroso, Kim Parker, and Jesse Bennett, "As Millennials Near 40, They're Approaching Family Life Differently than Previous Generations," Pew Research Center, May 27, 2020, https://www.pewresearch.org/social-trends/2020/05/27/as-millennials-near-40-theyre-approaching-family-life-differently-than-previous-generations/.

4. Ibid.

5. Mary Beth Franklin, "Dealing with Widows Requires Empathy and Patience," InvestmentNews, May 23, 2019, https://www.investmentnews.com/dealing-with-widows-requires-empathy-and-patience-79649.

6. Megan Leonhardt, "1 in 5 Millennials with Debt Expect to Die without Ever Paying It Off," CNBC, January 11, 2019, https://www.cnbc.com/2019/01/08/1-in-5-millennials-with-debt-expect-to-die-without-ever-paying-it-off.html.

7. Anna Sophia Martin, "The Undetected Influence of Generation X," *Forbes* magazine, September 13, 2016. https://www.forbes.com/sites/nextavenue/2016/09/13/the-undetected-influence-of-generation-x/?sh=21a931b11efb.

Chapter 24: Eight Habits of Wise Women Managing Money

1. Peter Anderson, "Bible Verses about Money: What Does the Bible Have To Say about Our Financial Lives?," Bible Money Matters, last edited October 8, 2021, https://www.biblemoneymatters.com/bible-verses-about-money-what-does-the-bible-have-to-say-about-our-financial-lives/.

Chapter 26: Legacy Giving: Gifts That Matter

1. Karen DeMasters, "Women Hold Majority of Personal Wealth, but Still Minorities in Advisory Field," *Financial Advisor*, March 25, 2020, https://www.fa-mag.com/news/women-need-to-lead-in-finances--consultant-says-54850.html.

2. Alisa Wolfson, "Why Women Give So Much More to Charity than Men," MarketWatch, October 26, 2018, https://www.marketwatch.com/story/why-women-give-so-much-more-to-charity-than-men-2018-10-26.

3. "Directions in Women's Giving 2012 Survey," Women Doing Well, accessed March 10, 2021, https://womendoingwell.org/resources/research/.

WI$E WOMEN
MANAGING MONEY

wisewomenmanagingmoney.com

Most women, at some time in their life, will manage their finances. Women in the United States control 51% of the wealth and direct most discretionary spending. Whether ready or not, prepared or unexpected, this is what we do.

We are a duo, mom (vintage) and daughter (JD and CFP), who know women want to do this well.
Financial know-how—practical.
Financial freedom—priceless.
Let's do this together!

WISE WOMEN MANAGING
MONEY

MORE FROM MIRIAM NEFF

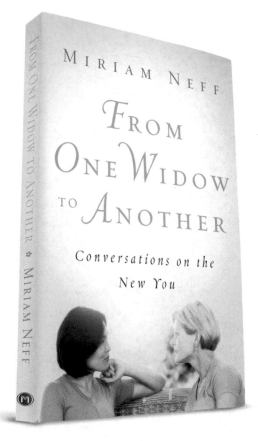

As Miriam Neff struggled to understand and accept her new role after her husband's death, she recognized the need for women to hear from other women about their experiences and what helped them transition to this new stage of life. *From One Widow to Another* offers practical advice for those facing the loss of a spouse. Drawing from her own loss, Neff walks with the reader through practical issues to a sense of encouragement.

978-0-8024-8784-1 | also available as an eBook

So much has changed...and yet, so much is exactly the same.

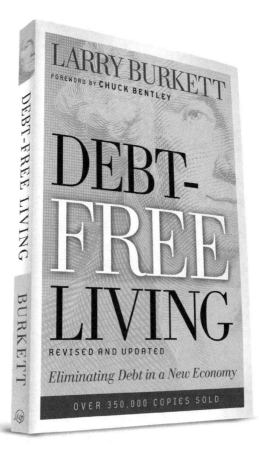

People often try managing their money
apart from God's plan. Bad plan.

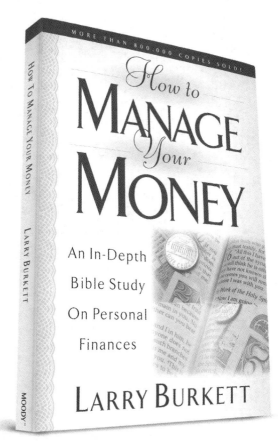